"This book traces the story of [barcode] portant episodes in the history c .... Pilgrims landed at Plymouth, Christians, informed by Calvin's missional theology, were planting churches and preaching the gospel in the country we now know as Brazil. This story has long been forgotten, suppressed, and even distorted by those who should have known better. I welcome this well-researched book, which sets the record straight."

Timothy George, Founding Dean, Beeson Divinity School; Chairman of the Board, The Colson Center for Christian Worldview

"Does a belief in sovereign grace stymie missions and evangelism? If that belief is rightly understood and rightly applied, the answer is an emphatic no. Haykin and Robinson skillfully present John Calvin's evangelistic zeal and channel it toward a new generation of Great Commission–minded pastors, teachers, and evangelists. I'm grateful for these men and this book, and pray that God will use it for the greater advance of the gospel and a greater harvest of souls."

Jason K. Allen, President, Midwestern Baptist Theological Seminary and College

"This book sets the record straight once and for all—John Calvin was a man consumed with the global proclamation of the gospel, the salvation of souls, and the discipleship of all nations. With historical integrity and pastoral insight, Haykin and Robinson demonstrate the beautiful harmony that exists between Calvinistic theology and a robust biblical missiology. Here is a call for the church to share in that same passionate pursuit."

Burk Parsons, Copastor, Saint Andrew's Chapel, Sanford, Florida; Editor, *Tabletalk* magazine

"Among the many myths surrounding Calvinism is the idea that it's anti-missions. Michael Haykin and Jeffrey Robinson draw into one place the many sources that demonstrate the tradition's missionary passion. They do so without defensive rhetoric—more out of a love for the Great Commission than for any party label. You don't have to be a Calvinist to find this story inspiring."

Michael Horton, J. Gresham Machen Professor of Systematic Theology and Apologetics, Westminster Seminary California; author, *Calvin on the Christian Life*

"The rehabilitation of Calvin (and his robust theology of divine sovereignty) as a leading figure in global missions is overdue, and few authors are qualified to do it with such enthusiasm and expertise as Haykin and Robinson. In *To the Ends of the Earth*, the perennial assertion that Calvin(ism) is destructive of evangelism and missions is convincingly shown to be entirely false—theologically and historically. Indeed, the very opposite is the case: Geneva proved to be a center of missionary endeavor and expansion. Read this book and then purchase several more copies to give to your friends. I cannot recommend it highly enough."

Derek W. H. Thomas, Minister of Preaching and Teaching, First Presbyterian Church, Columbia, South Carolina; Professor of Systematic Theology and Historical Theology, Reformed Theological Seminary, Atlanta

"For all the attention given to John Calvin, it boggles the mind that something so essential to him has gone largely unnoticed and unappreciated. Thank you, Drs. Haykin and Robinson, for introducing us to Calvin's missionary and evangelistic zeal. Let's hope it's contagious."

Stephen J. Nichols, President, Reformation Bible College; Chief Academic Officer, Ligonier Ministries

"The modern missionary movement did not begin *ex nihilo* in the late eighteenth century. To understand the thrust of contemporary global gospel advancement, one need understand that behind Fuller and Carey there were Edwards and Brainerd. And Edwards was the last theological bridge to classic English Puritanism. And the Puritans have their headwaters in Geneva. In this fine volume, readers will have many questions answered and many more questions raised, but a wonderful discovery will take place that I pray will stir many hearts to action in taking the gospel to the world."

Jason G. Duesing, Vice President of Strategic Initiatives and Assistant Professor of Historical Theology, Southwestern Baptist Theological Seminary

"Finally, a book that not only removes the myth of a lack of mission incentive in the Calvinist tradition, but also solidly and enthusiastically stimulates those inside and outside that tradition to get the message out."

Herman Selderhuis, Director, Refo500, The Netherlands

"Haykin and Robinson show convincingly that Calvinist commitment to the gospel of free grace has driven evangelism and missions for five hundred years. Not only does this book provide a much-needed reassessment of Calvin and missions, but it also extends its accounting through the Puritans, Jonathan Edwards, and Calvinist Baptists. In doing this, Haykin and Robinson provide a valuable resource for the church and a tract to motivate us to take the gospel to the ends of the earth in our own time as well."

Sean Michael Lucas, Senior Minister, The First Presbyterian Church, Hattiesburg, Mississippi; Associate Professor of Church History, Reformed Theological Seminary, Jackson

"Evangelism, missions, and prayer for the lost cannot long endure without a foundation in the doctrines of God's glory and sovereign grace. Michael Haykin and Jeffrey Robinson demonstrate through careful historical research that despite all claims to the contrary, Reformed truth has been a vital root feeding visionary and sacrificial efforts to reach the world with the gospel. May God use these thrilling accounts to magnify the glory of his grace, and to move many Christians to pour out their lives for the sake of Christ's kingdom in all lands."

Joel R. Beeke, President, Puritan Reformed Theological Seminary

TO THE
ENDS
OF THE
EARTH

CALVIN'S MISSIONAL VISION AND LEGACY

MICHAEL A. G. HAYKIN
AND C. JEFFREY ROBINSON SR.

WHEATON, ILLINOIS

To the Ends of the Earth: Calvin's Missional Vision and Legacy

Copyright © 2014 by Michael A. G. Haykin and Charles Jeffrey Robinson Sr.

Published by Crossway
>
1300 Crescent Street
Wheaton, Illinois 60187

Cover design: Jason Gabbert Design

First printing 2014

Printed in the United States of America

Trade paperback ISBN: 978-1-4335-2354-0
PDF ISBN: 978-1-4335-2365-6
Mobipocket ISBN: 978-1-4335-2366-3
ePub ISBN: 978-1-4335-2367-0

Library of Congress Cataloging-in-Publication Data
Haykin, Michael A. G.
    To the ends of the earth : Calvin's missional vision and
legacy / Michael A. G. Haykin and C. Jeffrey Robinson Sr.
        pages cm. — (Refo 500)
    Includes bibliographical references and index.
    ISBN 978-1-4335-2354-0 (tp)
    1. Calvin, Jean, 1509–1564. 2. Great Commission (Bible)
3. Missions—Theory. 4. Reformed Church—Doctrines.
I. Title.
BX9418.H37   2014
266'.42—dc23   2013041374

Crossway is a publishing ministry of Good News Publishers.

VP		24	23	22	21	20	19	18	17	16	15	14
15	14	13	12	11	10	9	8	7	6	5	4	3	2	1

To Kirk and Debbie Wellum,
for the joy of friendship and of being
co-laborers in the gospel,
and
to Thomas J. Nettles,
mentor, friend, and defender of gospel doctrines,
which Calvin held dear

If Calvinism is an enemy to missions and
evangelism, it is an enemy to the gospel itself.
The Great Commission and the task of evangelism
are assigned to every congregation and every believer.
The charge that Calvinism is opposed to evangelism
simply will not stick—it is a false argument. . . .
The great promise [of the gospel] is that whosoever calls
upon the name of the Lord shall be saved.

R. ALBERT MOHLER

Contents

Preface

Matthew 28:19–20, what is today often called the Great Commission, has had a fascinating history of reception. In the Patristic era, especially in the fourth century, it was used primarily as a text to support orthodox Trinitarianism.[1] During the eras of the Reformation and Puritanism, it was employed by both Anabaptists and Baptists to support their call for the baptism of believers only.[2] Then, in the late eighteenth century, it played a critical role in the galvanization of what is called the modern missionary movement.[3]

John Calvin (1509–1564), who is the subject of half of this book, interpreted the dominical command in Matthew 28 to pertain primarily to the apostles, who were thus commanded to fan out into the whole earth, "in order that by spreading the gospel wherever they can among the nations, they may raise up his [i.e., Christ's] Kingdom everywhere."[4] Calvin would have preferred to restrict the office and gift of apostle to the first-century church, but he conceded that sometimes the Lord has "at a later period raised up apostles, or at least evangelists in their place."[5] And if he were asked

---

[1] Michael A. G. Haykin, *Tri-Unity: An Essay on the Biblical Doctrine of God* (n.p.: NiceneCouncil.com, 2011), 17–26 passim.

[2] See, for example, Abraham Friesen, *Erasmus, the Anabaptists, and the Great Commission* (Grand Rapids: Eerdmans, 1998), and below, chap. 4.

[3] See, for example, William Carey, *An Enquiry into the Obligations of Christians to Use Means for the Conversion of the Heathens* (Leicester: Ann Ireland, 1792); and Michael A. G. Haykin, "Andrew Fuller on Mission: Text and Passion," in *Baptists and Mission: Papers from the Fourth International Conference on Baptist Studies,* ed. Ian M. Randall and Anthony R. Cross, Studies in Baptist History and Thought 29 (Milton Keynes, UK: Paternoster, 2007), 25–41.

[4] John Calvin, *Institutes of the Christian Religion,* ed. John T. McNeill, trans. Ford Lewis Battles (Philadelphia: Westminster, 1960), 2:1056 (4.3.4). See also Calvin's commentary on Matt. 28:19–20 and his *Commentary on the Epistle to the Ephesians* (Grand Rapids: Baker, 1999), 279.

[5] Calvin, *Institutes,* 2:1057 (4.3.4).

to give an example of such, Calvin would have pointed to Martin Luther (1483–1546), whom he once called "a distinguished apostle of Christ by whose ministry the light of the gospel has shone."[6]

Calvin's interpretation of Matthew 28:19–20 does not mean, however, that there was no place in his thinking, or practice, for missional activity. In fact, Calvin was confident that "the Kingdom established by the Apostles continued to advance and grow,"[7] and, therefore, God's people "must daily desire that God gathers churches unto himself from all parts of the earth" and "that he spread and increase them in number."[8] And as we shall see in what follows, Calvin's thinking is pervaded by rich missiological resources, as is the Puritan tradition that takes its rise from his thinking. Andrew F. Walls has recently sought to locate the roots of the modern missionary movement in seventeenth-century German Pietism.[9] This book seeks not to dispute this argument, but to maintain that, in their missional thinking, men like William Carey (1761–1834) and Samuel Pearce (1766–1799) also drew from a Calvinistic stream of thinking that they found first in Jonathan Edwards (1703–1758) and the Puritans, and which, regardless of whether they actually read Calvin, ultimately goes back to the French Reformer.

The first three chapters are thus devoted to looking at the exegetical foundations of Calvin's missional thought, his theology of mission, and two examples of his actual practice. Chapter 4 then looks at the seventeenth-century Puritans and Calvinistic Baptists, and finds clear evidence of substantial missionary longings. The next chapter looks at Jonathan Edwards, in some ways the last of the Puritans, as well as being a founding father of evangelicalism. And even as missionary activism has been a hallmark of the evangelical movement, so Edwards displays a similar mind-set. His grounding of missions in the matrix of prayer would bear fruit at the end of the eighteenth century, when men like Carey and Pearce

[6] John T. McNeill, in ibid., note 4.
[7] Andrew Buckler, *Jean Calvin et la mission de l'Eglise* (Lyon: Editions Olivétan, 2008), 57.
[8] Calvin, *Institutes*, 2:905 (3.20.42).
[9] Andrew F. Walls, "The Eighteenth-Century Protestant Missionary Awakening in Its European Context," in *Christian Missions and the Enlightenment*, ed. Brian Stanley (Grand Rapids: Eerdmans, 2001), 22–44.

took up his challenge to devote time in prayer for missions, which, in turn, led them to found the Baptist Missionary Society, the first of a host of similar, like-minded endeavors.

Taken together, the chapters of this book seek to lay to rest the charge that to be a Calvinist is to cease being missional. The leading subjects of this book are all Calvinists—and as shall be seen, all passionately missional.

Some of the material in this book has appeared elsewhere, and we are thankful for permission to use it here: to Reformation Heritage Books and *The Southern Baptist Journal of Theology* for sections of chapter 2;[10] to the Banner of Truth Trust for material in chapter 5;[11] and to Joshua Press for a goodly amount of chapter 6.[12] Other areas of indebtedness have been acknowledged in footnotes in the course of the book.

---

[10] Michael A. G. Haykin, "Calvin and the Missionary Endeavor of the Church," in *Calvin for Today*, ed. Joel R. Beeke (Grand Rapids: Reformation Heritage, 2009), 169–79; and Haykin, "'A Sacrifice Well Pleasing to God': John Calvin and the Missionary Endeavor of the Church," *The Southern Baptist Journal of Theology* 13, no. 4 (Winter 2009): 36–43.

[11] Michael A. G. Haykin, "Advancing the Kingdom of Christ: Jonathan Edwards, the Missionary Theologian," *The Banner of Truth* 482 (November 2003): 2–10.

[12] Michael A. G. Haykin, *Joy Unspeakable and Full of Glory: The Piety of Samuel and Sarah Pearce* (Kitchener, ON: Joshua, 2012).

Introduction

The Rev. S. L. Morris, on the occasion of the four-hundredth anniversary of Calvin's birth in May 1909, told the General Assembly of the Presbyterian Church in the United States as it gathered in Savannah, Georgia, to mark the Reformer's birth, "Calvinism is the most potent agency in the evangelization of the world."[1] At the time, no one would have regarded Morris's affirmation as outlandish. Today, though, just over one hundred years later, his remark is the stuff of controversy and considered a complete oxymoron.

Calvinism's Bad Press

In the West in 2013, a sentiment opposite that of Morris's is more typically heard among evangelicals: "Calvinism is the enemy of world evangelization." Virtually every admirer of Calvin and his theology has heard the same refrain: Calvin, his fellow Reformers, and their theology were not, are not, and cannot be, logically or theologically, pro-missions or pro-evangelism. The critics and their critiques border on cliché, and most who delight in a theology of sovereign grace can recite them: the sixteenth-century Reformers had a poorly developed missiology; overseas missions were given no thought or attention; Calvinism's theology of an absolutely sovereign, choosing God has precious little to say to the lost and is anti-missions and opposed to evangelism.

John Calvin wished to be interred, upon his death, in an un-

---

[1] S. L. Morris, "The Relation of Calvin and Calvinism to Missions," in *Calvin Memorial Addresses*, ed. Benjamin B. Warfield et al. (1909; repr., Birmingham, AL: Solid Ground Christian Books, 2007), 133.

marked grave and asked that his family, church members, and intimate friends avoid any form of memorial service so that no cult of personality might spring up around him.[2] In his last will and testament, Calvin's instructions to those at his deathbed were similarly pithy, the language unadorned: "I desire that my body after my death be interred in the usual manner, to wait for the day of the blessed resurrection."[3] Nearly 450 years after his death, historians still do not know the location of Calvin's grave, and given his reputation in the twenty-first-century West, Calvin's anonymous resting place is likely best for all parties concerned. It is quite conceivable that knowledge of his burial location would only incite some of his opponents to make pilgrimage there so as to spit upon it.

John Calvin is a historical figure in desperate need of a public-relations makeover. Of all the Western church Reformers of the sixteenth century, none has been so consistently defamed, none so ruthlessly castigated in both his doctrine and his personality from his own time to the present. For scores of modern-day evangelicals, Calvin is the ultimate megalomaniac, a dark figure, a theological hall monitor, a figure fixated on a wrathful God whose life and doctrines stood firmly opposed to missions and evangelism.

Even the so-called new media of the twenty-first century has been commandeered to wage this perennial war on Calvin. Visitors to YouTube, the Internet dumping ground for everything from home movies depicting stupid pet tricks to Duran Duran videos, will find numerous broadside attacks on John Calvin and his theology. The unsubtle titles include, "How to Defeat Calvinism," "All of Calvinism Refuted by One Verse" (by one who apparently thinks Arminians hail from the Eurasian republic of Armenia), "Why I Am Not a Five-Point Calvinist," "Burn in Hell, John Calvin, Burn," "Calvinism Creeping In," and "Sovereign Grace Is a Heresy." Even the televangelist Jimmy Swaggart took an oft-quoted swipe at Calvin, declaring that the Genevan Reformer was responsible for caus-

---

[2] Bruce Gordon, *Calvin* (New Haven, CT: Yale University Press, 2009), 336–37.

[3] John Calvin, "Last Will and Testament of Master John Calvin," in *Tracts and Letters*, ed. Jules Bonnet, trans. Marcus Robert Gilchrist, 7 vols. (1858; repr., Edinburgh: Banner of Truth, 2009), 7:366.

ing "untold numbers to be lost—or seriously hindered—in their spiritual walk and relationship with God."[4] If only his contemporaries had been so kind to Calvin! Jérôme-Hermès Bolsec (died c. 1584), a contemporary of Calvin and one-time Protestant advocate, published a biography of the Reformer after returning to the Roman Catholic Church, which the twentieth-century Calvin scholar Richard Stauffer termed "nothing more than a vile tract." In it, Bolsec vilified the Reformer as "ambitious, presumptuous, arrogant, cruel, evil, vindictive, avaricious, and, above all, ignorant."[5] Once he commenced, Bolsec kept the fists flying. For him, Calvin was "a greedy man, . . . an imposter who claimed he could resurrect the dead, . . . a gadabout, a Sodomite," an outcast of God.[6]

Time has done little to temper public opinion of John Calvin. In 1951, André Favre-Dorsaz wrote what Stauffer called "the most destructive book about Calvin with which I am acquainted."[7] Favre-Dorsaz contrasted Calvin with Ignatius Loyola (1491–1556), founder of the Society of Jesus, calling the Reformer "an acid, negative person" who was a "withdrawn, embittered and unfeeling, coldly committed pessimist; an uneasy, worried, anguished man, alternately sympathetic and cruel; proud, a repressed sentimentalist, truly sadistic; a sick man . . . and . . . a dictator."[8] Austrian novelist Stefan Zweig (1881–1942) considered Calvin interchangeable with Adolf Hitler, while Oscar Pfister, Sigmund Freud's Swiss theological admirer, wrote off Calvin as a "compulsive-neurotic who transformed the God of Love as experienced and taught by Jesus into a compulsive character, a fanatic of hateful cruelty, bearing absolutely diabolical traits."[9] More recently, Will Durant, coauthor with his

---

[4] Jimmy Swaggart, quoted by Allen C. Guelzo, "A Life of John Calvin," review of *A Study of the Shaping of Western Culture*, by Alister E. McGrath (Oxford: Blackwell, 1990), *Touchstone*, accessed at http://www.touchstonemag.com/archives/article.php?id=05-04-038-b.

[5] Quoted in Richard Stauffer, *The Humanness of John Calvin* (1971; repr., Birmingham, AL: Solid Ground Christian Books, 2008), 20.

[6] Quoted in ibid.

[7] Ibid., 25.

[8] Ibid., 25–26.

[9] Matthias Freudenberg, "Calvin's Reception in the Twentieth Century," trans. Randi H. Lundell, in Herman J. Selderhuis, *The Calvin Handbook* (Grand Rapids: Eerdmans, 2009), 503; Allen Guelzo, "Review: *A Life of John Calvin: A Study of the Shaping of Western Culture*, by Alister E. McGrath," *Touchstone* 5, no. 4 (Fall 1992), accessed September 14, 2013, http://www.touchstonemag.com/archives/article.php?id=05-04-038-b.

wife of a multivolume series on the history of Western civilization, offered criticism of Calvin that seems unfit for a historian: "We shall always find it hard to love the man, John Calvin, who darkened the human soul with the most absurd and blasphemous conception of God in all the long and honored history of nonsense."[10]

The Missiology of the Reformers

If John Calvin the man is viewed as something of a theological despot in the Western mind, his theology, particularly as it relates to the area of soteriology and its link to missions and evangelism, has fared even worse. Reformed theology, which has become identified with Calvin's name—though, to tell the truth, his thinking is only one of a number of springs that produced this theological stream—emphasizes the absolute sovereignty of God in both creation and redemption. This sovereignty entails the doctrines of unconditional election and particular redemption, subscription to which, some have argued, renders Calvin and those who share his theology as logical nonstarters in the church's missionary task. It has often been maintained that the sixteenth-century Reformers had a poorly developed missiology and that overseas missions to non-Christians was an area to which they gave little thought. Yes, this argument runs, the Reformers rediscovered the apostolic gospel, but they had no vision to spread it to the uttermost parts of the earth.[11] Historian Gustav Warneck, for example, has painted Calvin as missiologically anemic because of his belief in the doctrines of predestination and election:

> We miss in the Reformers, not only missionary action, but even the idea of missions, in the sense in which we understand them today. And this not only because the newly discovered world

---

[10] Quoted in Frank A. James III, "Calvin the Evangelist," *Reformed Quarterly* 20, no. 2/3 (Fall 2001), accessed September 14, 2013, http://rq.rts.edu/fall01/james.html. In a mid-twentieth-century series of books designed for high school students, one finds a similar evaluation of Calvin. His "doctrines were harsh" and as a result "there was little joy in Calvin's church." Johanna Johnston and James L. Steffensen, *Reformation and Exploration*, vol. 8 of *The Universal History of the World* (New York: Golden, n.d.), 641.

[11] See Kenneth J. Stewart, "Calvinism and Missions: The Contested Relationship Revisited," *Themelios* 34, no. 1 (April 2009): 63–78.

across the sea lay almost wholly beyond the range of their vision, though that reason had some weight, but because fundamental theological views hindered them from giving their activity and even their thoughts a missionary direction.[12]

And Ruth A. Tucker has argued the same: Calvin's doctrine of predestination "made missions extraneous if God had already chosen those he would save."[13]

Possibly the very first author to raise this question about early Protestantism's failure to apply itself to missionary work was the Roman Catholic theologian and controversialist Robert Bellarmine (1542–1621). Bellarmine argued that one of the marks of a true church is its continuity with the missionary passion of the apostles. In his mind, Roman Catholicism's missionary activity was indisputable and this supplied a strong support for its claim to stand in solidarity with the apostles. As Bellarmine maintained:

> In this one century the Catholics have converted many thousands of heathens in the new world. Every year a certain number of Jews are converted and baptized at Rome by Catholics who adhere in loyalty to the Bishop of Rome. . . . The Lutherans compare themselves to the apostles and the evangelists; yet though they have among them a very large number of Jews, and in Poland and Hungary have the Turks as their near neighbors, they have hardly converted so much as a handful.[14]

This characterization, though, fails to account for the complexity of the historical context of the Reformation. First of all, to answer both a Roman Catholic apologist like Bellarmine and a Protestant missiologist like Warneck, in the earliest years of the Reformation

---

[12] Gustav Warneck, *History of Protestant Missions,* trans. G. Robson from the 8th German ed. (Edinburgh: Oliphant Anderson & Ferrier, 1906), 9. Warneck's opinion has been influential on subsequent missiological reflection. See, for example, David Allen, "Preaching for a Great Commission Resurgence," in *The Great Commission Resurgence: Fulfilling God's Mandate in Our Time,* ed. Chuck Lawless and Adam W. Greenway (Nashville, TN: B&H, 2010), 286.

[13] Ruth A. Tucker, *From Jerusalem to Irian Jaya: A Biographical History of Christian Missions* (Grand Rapids: Zondervan, 1983), 67.

[14] Robert Bellarmine, *Controversiae,* book 4, as quoted in Stephen Neill, *A History of Christian Missions* (Harmondsworth, UK: Penguin, 1964), 221.

none of the major Protestant bodies possessed significant naval and maritime resources to take the gospel outside of the bounds of Europe. The Iberian Catholic kingdoms of Spain and Portugal, on the other hand, who were the acknowledged leaders among missions-sending regions at this time, had such resources aplenty. Moreover, the Roman Catholic missionary endeavors were often indistinguishable from imperialist ventures. It is noteworthy that other Roman Catholic nations of Europe, like Poland and Hungary, also lacked sea-going capabilities and evidenced no more cross-cultural missionary concern at that time than did Lutheran Saxony or Reformed Zürich. It is thus plainly wrong to make the simplistic assertion that Roman Catholic nations were committed to overseas missions whereas no Protestant power was so committed.[15]

Second, it is vital to recognize that, as Scott Hendrix has shown, the Reformation was the attempt to "make European culture more Christian than it had been. It was, if you will, an attempt to re-root faith, to re-christianize Europe."[16] In the eyes of the Reformers, this program involved two accompanying convictions. First, they considered what passed for Christianity in late medieval Europe as sub-Christian at best, pagan at worst. As Calvin put it in his *Reply to Sadoleto* (1539):

> The light of divine truth had been extinguished, the Word of God buried, the virtue of Christ left in profound oblivion, and the pastoral office subverted. Meanwhile, impiety so stalked abroad that almost no doctrine of religion was pure from admixture, no ceremony free from error, no part, however minute, of divine worship untarnished by superstition.[17]

And in the *Institutes* Calvin commented that in the churches of Europe, "Christ lies hidden, half buried, the gospel overthrown,

[15] Stewart, "Calvinism and Missions," 67–68.
[16] Scott Hendrix, "Rerooting the Faith: The Reformation as Re-Christianization," *Church History* 69 (2000): 561. See also his *Recultivating the Vineyard: The Reformation Agendas of Christianization* (Louisville, KY: Westminster John Knox, 2004); and Michael Parsons, *Calvin's Preaching on the Prophet Micah: The 1550–1551 Sermons in Geneva* (Lewiston, NY: Edwin Mellen, 2006), 189–93.
[17] John Calvin and Jacopo Sadoleto, *A Reformation Debate*, ed. John C. Olin (Grand Rapids: Baker, 1976), 74–75.

piety scattered, the worship of God nearly wiped out. In them, briefly, everything is so confused that there we see the face of Babylon rather than that of the Holy City of God."[18] And so, the Reformers did indeed view their task as a missionary one, for they were planting true Christian churches.[19]

Calvinism and Missions

Some recent evangelical scholars have also painted Calvin's theology as an unbiblical system that neutralizes the Great Commission. In an article in the *Texas Baptist Standard* newspaper, the late William R. Estep, a noted historian on the Reformation period, sounded the alarm to awaken his fellow Southern Baptists to the growing menace of "the new Calvinism." Should the Southern Baptist Convention embrace Calvinistic soteriology in wholesale fashion, Estep—ironically borrowing a phrase from Andrew Fuller (1754–1815), English Baptist theologian and ardent Calvinist—predicted the denomination would become "a perfect dunghill in American society."[20] Why such a blanket dismissal by such an able historian? Estep chronicled five problems with Calvinistic soteriology, arguing centrally that it denies many salvation passages in the New Testament and that its God resembles Allah, the God of Islam, more than the gracious God of Christianity. Chief among his concerns is that, Estep argued, unconditional election is "logically . . . anti-missionary" and renders the Great Commission "meaningless."[21] Calvin's soteriology means that every person is "programmed" to be damned or saved, and it makes "a person into a puppet on a string," he further argued.[22]

Not everyone within the great cloud of historic and contemporary witnesses, however, views Calvin and his theology as a great enemy of missions and evangelism. In a recent work, evangelical

---

[18] Calvin, *Institutes*, 2:1053 (4.2.12). See also *Institutes*, 4.2.11.
[19] Hendrix, "Rerooting the Faith," 558–68.
[20] William Estep, "Calvinizing Southern Baptists," *Texas Baptist Standard* (March 26, 1997). This article was substantially reprinted as "Doctrines Lead to 'Dunghill' Prof Warns," *The Founders Journal* 29 (Summer 1997), accessed September 14, 2013, http://www.founders.org/journal/fj29/article1.html.
[21] Estep, "Calvinizing Southern Baptists."
[22] Ibid.

historian Kenneth J. Stewart forcefully argues that Calvin and the Reformed tradition have by no means neglected world missions and evangelism. Calvin was deeply concerned about the salvation of the lost, which, along with the recovery of biblical worship, was one of the major goals of the Reformation.[23] Writes Stewart:

> Late-twentieth-century prognosticators about an assumed dampening effect of Calvinism on missions have therefore made their pronouncements rashly. Alarmist statements, made in these last decades in the face of the current resurgence of interest in Reformed theology, surely ought to give way to more careful assessments if missions history is to be trusted. If it is true that *all* branches of the Christian family might have done more for missions, then it is also true that this branch has been "in missionary harness" as long as any expression of Protestantism.[24]

David B. Calhoun has also argued that Calvin and his fellow Reformers were by no means guilty of missional absenteeism. Rather, the Reformers in general and Calvin in particular provided the theological framework that energized global missions. One of the primary themes in Calvin's mission theology, Calhoun asserts, was the spread of the kingdom of God:

> Calvin, along with the other Reformers, did a great service to missions generally by his earnest proclamation of the gospel and his re-ordering of the church according to Biblical requirements. The missionary message and the structure of missions are two primary concerns which can be informed by his insights. More specifically, however, Calvin's teaching concerning the universality of Christ's kingdom and the responsibility of Christians in extending the kingdom have immense missionary implications.[25]

---

[23] In *Ten Myths about Calvinism: Recovering the Breadth of the Reformed Tradition* (Downers Grove, IL: InterVarsity, 2011), Stewart debunks two popular misconceptions surrounding Calvin's theology: that it is anti-missions and that it tends toward a rejection of revival and spiritual awakening.

[24] Ibid., 147.

[25] David B. Calhoun, "John Calvin: Missionary Hero or Missionary Failure?," *Presbyterion* 5, no. 1 (Spring 1979): 16–17.

Calvin's theology was actually no impediment to his own missionary activities, but, rather, served as a catalyst for transforming Geneva into a hub of missionary activity where Reformed ministers were trained and sent out to proclaim the gospel throughout Europe and beyond, especially France and Brazil. Despite his reputation, Calvin was no stay-at-home theologian, and his theology was by no means a do-nothing worldview. Philip E. Hughes concurs:

> Calvin's Geneva was something very much more than a haven and a school. It was not a theological ivory tower that lived to itself and for itself, oblivious of its responsibility in the gospel to the needs of others. Human vessels were equipped and refitted in this haven, not to be status symbols like painted yachts safely moored at a fashionable marina, but that they might launch out into the surrounding ocean of the world's need, bravely facing every storm and peril that awaited them in order to bring the light of Christ's gospel to those who were in the ignorance and darkness from which they themselves had originally come. . . . Geneva became a dynamic center or nucleus from which the vital missionary energy it generated radiated out into the world beyond.[26]

Likewise, it can be argued that Calvin's theology has served as a great engine that has empowered the church since the Reformation in its task of world evangelization. One can point, for example, to Jonathan Edwards, America's greatest theologian, who preached a decidedly Reformed soteriology. Edwards's preaching animated the First Great Awakening in the 1740s in America, and he developed a strategy for prayer that was crucial in later periods of revival and missionary endeavor in the eighteenth century. In fact, he himself later served as a missionary to the Indians on the rough and rugged frontier of western Massachusetts.[27] Or one can single out Samuel Pearce, an unabashed Calvinist, who was a domestic "rope

---

[26] Philip E. Hughes, "John Calvin: Director of Missions," in *The Heritage of John Calvin*, ed. John H. Bratt (Grand Rapids: Eerdmans, 1973), 44–45.
[27] See below, chap. 5.

holder" for William Carey and his colleagues in their mission to Bengal and who exemplified a Calvinistic Baptist missionary spirituality.[28] Largely because of Andrew Fuller's biography of Pearce, the mission-minded piety of Pearce came to be regarded as exemplary not only by the Calvinistic Baptist community to which he belonged but also by other evangelical traditions of the day, such as the Methodists. The lives and ministries of these two men and countless other Calvinists[29] go a long way toward disproving the popular notion that Calvin's theology severs the missiological and evangelistic nerve of the gospel.

But why is there so much reticence about the missional credentials and motivations of Calvin and his theology? Joel Beeke attributes this attitude toward Calvin and his theology to several factors, including "a failure to study Calvin's writings prior to drawing conclusions, a failure to understand Calvin's own view of evangelism within his own historical context and/or preconceived doctrinal notions about Calvin and his theology."[30] Largely, it is attributable to theological and historical naïveté and fear.

Whatever the factors that call into question the missionary and evangelistic commitments of Calvin and the other Reformers, an examination of Calvin's most important writings reveals a focused concern for the recovery of the purity of the gospel with the salvation of souls as the final end. Alongside the majority of believers throughout the history of the church, Calvin affirmed election and predestination as doctrines articulated by the Word of God. And yet, for Calvin, it was necessary that the church undergo reformation to recover the gospel and bring the good news of God's redeeming love in Christ Jesus to those who for centuries had walked in the darkness of a severely deficient Roman Catholic gospel. Calvin made these core concerns clear in his treatise on the necessity of reforming the church, addressed to Charles V, Holy

---

[28] See below, chap. 6.
[29] See the overview in chap. 4.
[30] Joel R. Beeke, "John Calvin, Teacher and Practitioner of Evangelism," in *Puritan Reformed Spirituality* (Grand Rapids: Reformation Heritage, 2004), 54.

Roman emperor, at the Fourth Diet of Speyer in 1544. After setting forth the recovery of the pure worship of God as the first aim of the Reformation, Calvin expressed as a second fundamental goal a rediscovery of "knowledge of the source from which salvation is to be obtained," a teaching he called "the second principal branch of Christian doctrine."[31] Calvin maintained that human depravity, the unmerited grace of God in Christ, and the exclusivity of *sola fide* in salvation had been twisted by the superstitions of Rome to such a degree that fallen men and women saw neither their captivity to sin's dark night nor the unilateral sovereign grace that must shine light into blackened hearts if they would be rescued.[32] Ultimately, Calvin's concern was that the eclipse of the gospel imperiled human souls.

For Calvin, the inextricably related truths of the pure worship of God and the salvation of souls were the two great concerns of the Reformation. It is historically and theologically naive to charge Calvin and his fellow Reformers with lacking a desire for the salvation of souls and failing to possess a concern for the nations. This was the Reformers' chief concern in seeking to recover pure worship and the pure gospel from what Martin Luther called its "Babylonian captivity" to the unbiblical teachings of the Roman Catholic Church. The present work will demonstrate that Calvin, in his writings and by his own missionary activities, was decidedly pro-missions and pro-evangelism. Considered together, Calvin's *Institutes of the Christian Religion*, his biblical commentaries, his sermons and other writings, and the system of theology expressed in them paint a picture of a man who understood that the Great Commission given by Christ in Matthew 28 remains in force and is the obligation of every Christian. For Calvin, the Reformation and its mission represented a recovery of the pure gospel of God, who is on mission to expand his kingdom through the salvation of sinners by the atoning work of Christ on Calvary.

---

[31] John Calvin, *The Necessity of Reforming the Church*, in *Tracts and Letters*, trans. Henry Beveridge, 7 vols. (1844; repr., Edinburgh: Banner of Truth, 2009), 1:133.
[32] Ibid., 1:134–35.

Calvin's theology of sovereign grace, complete with its doctrines of predestination and election, would ultimately bear fruit in that major wing of the modern missions movement that commenced with William Carey. And as we shall see, his soteriology served as foundational for the doctrinal beliefs of others, like Jonathan Edwards and Samuel Pearce, by which they were motivated to take the gospel to the nations. It may be the case that the Calvinism of the men studied in this book is not biblical—though we would beg to disagree—but after one reads about the missionary passion of these Reformed pastor-theologians, may it not be said that being Calvinistic and being missional are mutually exclusive!

1

"For God So Loved the World"

JOHN CALVIN'S MISSIONAL EXEGESIS

Calvin as a Biblical Theologian

The great delight of John Calvin's heart was studying and teaching Holy Scripture. Above all else, he was a student and preacher of God's Word. While Calvin's critics—and they have been myriad—have accused him of everything from inventing predestination to insisting upon the damnation of infants, one accusation that sticks is that Calvin was a lover of the Bible. In his commentaries, theological writings, and sermons, Calvin sought to say what the Bible says. Where God's Word speaks to an issue, Calvin sought to address it. From his own voluminous written analysis of Scripture, Calvin sought to go as far and high and wide and deep as God's Word—but no further. Thus, he wrote much about salvation, sin, eternal damnation, God's sovereignty, prayer, the wrath of God, reprobation, and yes, predestination; he wrote and preached and taught about these topics—controversial and noncontroversial—because the Bible addresses them all.

One senses the depth of his affection for the Bible in the preface to his commentary on the book of Psalms, written toward the end of his life in 1557:

> If the reading of these my commentaries confer as much benefit on the Church of God as I myself have reaped advantage from the composition of them, I shall have no reason to regret that I have undertaken this work. . . . The varied and resplendid [i.e., resplendent] riches which are contained in this treasury it is no easy matter to express in words; so much so, that I well know that whatever I shall be able to say will be far from approaching the excellence of the subject.[1]

Calvin's commentaries were, as David L. Puckett points out, an extension of his spoken ministry as a doctor of theology and were mostly taken from lectures delivered to ministerial candidates.[2] Calvin published his first biblical commentary on the Pauline epistle of Romans in 1540 during his ministry in Strasbourg. After completing the Romans commentary, Calvin took a six-year hiatus from publishing his expositional works. But between 1546 and 1551, Calvin was prolific, publishing verse-by-verse expositions of 1 and 2 Corinthians, Galatians, Ephesians, Philippians, Colossians, 1 and 2 Thessalonians, 1 and 2 Timothy, Titus, Philemon, Hebrews, 1 and 2 Peter, James, 1 John, and Jude.[3] Over the next four years, through 1555, Calvin published his two-part commentary on Acts, a commentary on John, and a harmony of the Synoptic Gospels. The only New Testament books for which Calvin did not release commentaries were 2 and 3 John and Revelation.[4] Calvin published his lectures on the Old Testament after completing the series on the New Testament and was in the midst of his work in the prophet Ezekiel when his diseased body forced the Reformer to his deathbed in 1564.[5]

---

[1] Preface to John Calvin, *Commentary on the Book of Psalms*, trans. James Anderson, vol. 1 (Grand Rapids: Eerdmans, 1949), xxxv–xxxvi.

[2] David L. Puckett, "John Calvin as Teacher," *The Southern Baptist Journal of Theology* 13, no. 4 (Winter 2009): 47.

[3] Ibid.

[4] T. H. L. Parker, *John Calvin: A Biography* (Philadelphia: Westminster, 1975), 106–7.

[5] Ibid. For a table outlining Calvin's teaching and preaching schedule between 1555 and 1564, see Andrew Buckler, *Jean Calvin et la mission de l'Eglise* (Lyon: Editions Olivétan, 2008), 217.

Calvin was also a systematic theologian. When he was twenty-six years old, he drafted the first edition of what would become his magnum opus, the *Institutes of the Christian Religion*. Five Latin editions followed the first, 1536 edition, culminating in the final edition in 1559. Nearly five hundred years later, Calvin's *Institutes* is considered by many to be one of the finest systematic theologies ever written, and it remains the most influential and complete defense of the Reformation to arise from the pen of the magisterial Reformers. Calvin scholar John T. McNeill argued that Calvin's *Institutes* is "one of the few books that have profoundly affected the course of history."[6] Similarly, the American church historian Philip Schaff wrote, "This book is the masterpiece of a precocious genius of commanding intellectual and spiritual depth and power. It is one of the few truly classical productions in the history of theology, and has given its author the double title of the Aristotle and Thomas Aquinas of the Reformed Church."[7] B. B. Warfield saw the *Institutes* as "supplying for the first time the constructive basis for the Reformation movement," a work that, for the first time in the history of the church, "drew in outline the plan of a complete structure of Christian Apologetics."[8]

While most think of Calvin's *Institutes* as a tour de force of Reformed thought (an accurate assessment), it is also a work that pulsates with concern for a lost and dying world, a world that profoundly needs to hear the message of God's redeeming love in Jesus Christ. Yes, the *Institutes* exposits in great detail the Bible's teaching on predestination and election, as expected since Calvin found those doctrines clearly established in the Bible; but it does so with a full awareness and expression of both the absolute sovereignty of God and the full responsibility of humanity. Thus, Calvin makes plain that the chief end of gospel proclamation and theological engagement is its service in the *missio dei*, the mission of God: to glorify himself through the salvation of sinful mankind. Thus,

---

[6] John T. McNeill, *The History and Character of Calvinism* (New York: Oxford University Press, 1967), 119.

[7] Philip Schaff, *History of the Christian Church*, 8 vols. (Grand Rapids: Eerdmans, 1953), 8:329.

[8] B. B. Warfield, "The Knowledge of God," in *The Works of Benjamin B. Warfield*, vol. 5, *Calvin and Calvinism* (Grand Rapids: Baker, 2000), 30.

election is secret and beyond humankind's ability to know. This being the case, we must pray for the conversion of all people, as Calvin wrote:

> The prayer of the Christian ought to be conformed to this rule in order that it may be in common and embrace all who are his brothers in Christ: not only those whom he presently sees and recognizes as such, but all people who dwell on earth. For what the Lord has determined regarding them is beyond our knowing, except that we ought to wish and hope for the best for them.[9]

Calvin was a theologian whose theology animated and did not undermine such praying for the salvation of all people, which will be the focus of a section later in this chapter.

The chapter will examine the fruit of Calvin's labors as an exegete of the Bible, as a theologian, and as a preacher of Scripture, with particular attention to Calvin's commentaries, the *Institutes of the Christian Religion*, and his sermons. The key "problem" texts of Scripture that have led opponents of Calvin to brand him "anti-missional" and "non-evangelistic" will be analyzed, as well as Calvin's approach to such matters as the universal call of the gospel in light of his doctrine of predestination. The picture that will emerge will reveal an approach to Scripture and theology that was clearly pro-missions and pro-evangelism. While Calvin was a first-generation Reformer concerned more directly with purifying the church than birthing a worldwide missions movement, his interpretation of the Bible and understanding of theology were consistent with a free and uninhibited proclamation of the gospel for the salvation of the lost.

First, this chapter will examine the so-called "universal" texts that many have used through the ages to expose Calvin as a theologian at odds with missions and evangelism. We will also examine the most prominent among the so-called Calvinistic texts that address salvation in terms of election and predestination, such as

---

[9] John Calvin, *Institutes of the Christian Religion* (1536), quoted in Elsie McKee, "Calvin and Praying for 'All People Who Dwell on Earth,'" *Interpretation* 63, no. 2 (April 2009): 130.

Ephesians 1 and Romans 9, among others. In addition to Calvin's sermons and the *Institutes*, the research will also draw from some of Calvin's important polemical works, including his debates with Albert Pighius (c. 1490–1542), Sebastian Castellio (1515–1563), and others on predestination, the bondage of the will, and the providence of God.

Calvin on the "Universal" Texts

Many of Calvinism's critics view the "all" passages in Scripture as the Achilles' heel of the system of theology most closely associated with the teaching of John Calvin. The logic goes like this: If the Bible says that God desires the salvation of every single person without exception, and he invites every single person without exception to receive saving grace, then Christians who believe doctrines such as election, predestination, and particular atonement cannot honestly call on sinners to repent and trust in Christ for salvation. In an attempt to refute Calvin's theology, many call upon what they consider an indicting series of "Arminian" verses, including Ezekiel 18:23, Matthew 23:37, John 3:16, 1 Timothy 2:4, and 2 Peter 3:9, to show such inconsistent thinking within Calvinism. One such critic was the late William Estep, the American Baptist historian quoted in the introduction to this work, who argued thus against Calvinism: "Calvinism appears to deny John 3:16, John 1:12, Romans 1:16, Romans 10:9–10, Ephesians 2:8–10, and numerous other passages of scripture that indicate . . . that salvation comes to those who respond to God's grace in faith."[10] While Calvin is usually best remembered for his articulation of the biblical doctrine of predestination, the Reformer did not see a call to the unconverted as inconsistent with the doctrines of God's secret choosing of a people before the foundation of the world. For the sake of biblical chronology, let us begin in the Old Testament with two texts in the prophet Ezekiel.

---

[10] William Estep, "Calvinizing Southern Baptists," *Texas Baptist Standard* (March 26, 1997). This article was substantially reprinted as "Doctrines Lead to 'Dunghill' Prof Warns," *The Founders Journal* 29 (Summer 1997), accessed September 14, 2013, http://www.founders.org/journal/fj29/article1.html.

"Have I Any Pleasure in the Death of the Wicked?"

In his comments on Ezekiel 18:23 ("Have I any pleasure in the death of the wicked, declares the Lord GOD, and not rather that he should turn from his way and live?"), Calvin affirmed that there is one sense in which God, according to his eternal will, desires the salvation of all men and women even while God predestines every person who will ever be saved.[11] This text, Calvin argued, makes clear that God calls all people without exception to salvation. During Old Testament times, the prophets called God's people to repentance and faith, and the call was without respect of persons. In the same way, the gospel goes forth to all people without exception in the new covenant. Though Calvin certainly affirmed election and predestination, there is nothing in those doctrines that hinders the prophet or preacher from demanding universal repentance.

In this text, Calvin argued that Ezekiel is calling people to repentance, and, while aware of the reality of predestination, the prophet is not speaking of God's secret purpose of election. Thus, Calvin maintained, there is no contradiction between the two doctrines—God's general call to sinners and his choosing of a people for salvation—both of which clearly appear in the Bible. Calvin chose to let the biblical tension between divine election and the free offer of the gospel stand without trying to solve what he calls elsewhere "an unfathomable mystery." While many throughout history will refuse God's overtures of grace, thus confirming God's secret election of some to salvation, Calvin saw no reason whatsoever to withhold the offer of God's redeeming love in Christ from any person. If one genuinely repents, God will receive him, Calvin asserted.

> We hold, then, that God does not will the death of a sinner, since he calls all equally to repentance and promises himself prepared to receive them if they only seriously repent. If any one should object—then there is no election of God, by which he has predestinated a fixed number to salvation, the answer is at hand. The prophet does not here speak of God's secret coun-

---

[11] For an examination of Calvin's thoughts on the "two wills of God," see below.

sel, but only recalls miserable men from despair, that they may apprehend the hope of pardon, and repent and embrace the offered salvation. If anyone again objects—this is making God act with duplicity, the answer is ready, that God always wishes the same thing, though by different ways, and in a manner inscrutable to us. Although, therefore, God's will is simple, yet great variety is involved in it, as far as our senses are concerned. Besides, it is not surprising that our eyes should be blinded by intense light, so that we cannot certainly judge how God wishes all to be saved, and yet has devoted all the reprobate to eternal destruction, and wishes them to perish.[12]

A similar verse that appears several chapters later in Ezekiel seems to stand at odds with the eternal decrees of God: "As I live, declares the Lord GOD, I have no pleasure in the death of the wicked, but that the wicked turn from his way and live; turn back, turn back from your evil ways, for why will you die, O house of Israel?" (Ezek. 33:11). In the *Institutes*, Calvin understood both Ezekiel 18:23 and 33:11 as setting forth the grace of God in the midst of Israel's spiritual adultery. The prophets, whose messages Calvin ultimately interpreted through a christological lens, promise the light of God's grace to even the darkest of rebels. God's promises are good news of mercy to God's people in both the old and new covenants. For Calvin, grace and not sin will have the final word:

> The prophets are full of promises of this kind, which offer mercy to a people [Israel] though they be covered with infinite crimes. What graver iniquity is there than rebellion? . . . Surely, there can be no other feeling in him who affirms that he does not desire the death of the sinner, but rather that he be converted and live [Ezek. 18:23, 32; 33:11]. Accordingly, when Solomon dedicated the Temple, he intended it also to be used so that thereby the prayers offered to obtain pardon of sins might be answered.[13]

---

[12] John Calvin, *Commentaries on the First Twenty Chapters of the Book of the Prophet Ezekiel*, trans. Thomas Myers (Grand Rapids: Baker, 1996), 247, word order slightly modernized.

[13] John Calvin, *Institutes of the Christian Religion*, ed. John T. McNeill, trans. Ford Lewis Battles (Philadelphia: Westminster, 1960), 2:1038 (4.1.25).

"For God So Loved the World, That He Gave His Only Son"

The Ezekiel passages are often quoted in refutation of Calvin's doctrine of predestination, but the most prevalent verse employed against Calvin and Calvinism is typically the first passage a child learns in Vacation Bible School, John 3:16: "For God so loved the world, that he gave his only son, that whoever believes in him should not perish but have eternal life." This is undoubtedly the text most often quoted to refute Calvinistic expressions of the doctrines of election and predestination. Calvin, however, as the original "Calvinist," did not stumble over the collective or universal words in the text. Contrary to popular opinion about the Reformer, he affirmed both God's universal love for humanity and the universal offer of the gospel that must be made to all sinners without exception:

> The whole substance of our salvation is not to be sought anywhere else than in Christ, and so we must see by what means Christ flows to us, and why he was offered as our Savior. Both points are clearly told us here—that faith in Christ quickens all, and that Christ brought life because the heavenly Father does not wish the human race he loves to perish.[14]

The phrase "whoever believes" is often used as proof that Calvin's theology of God's sovereign choice in salvation is fallacious; a consistent follower of Calvin's theology should not invite all sinners to salvation, some insist. Calvin, however, had no such scruples with the language, but affirmed the universal invitation of sinners to Christ in his comments on John 3:16:

> The outstanding thing about faith is it delivers us from eternal destruction. For he [John] especially wanted to say that although we seem to have been born for death deliverance is offered to us by faith in Christ so that we must not fear the death

---

[14] John Calvin, *The Gospel according to St John 1–10*, trans. T. H. L. Parker (Grand Rapids: Eerdmans, 1959), 73.

which otherwise threatens us. And he has used a general term, both to invite indiscriminately all to share in life and to cut off every excuse from unbelievers. Such is also the significance of the term "world" which he had used before. For although there is nothing in the world deserving of God's favor, he nevertheless shows he is favorable to the whole world when he calls all without exception to faith in Christ, which is indeed an entry into life.[15]

Has Calvin abandoned his belief in divine election? Certainly not. After examining the word "world" in John 3:16 and establishing the general call of the gospel, which goes out to all indiscriminately, Calvin set forth the Bible's position on the complementarity of God's sovereignty and human responsibility. Many may be called to repent and believe in Christ through gospel proclamation, but only those whom God enables to come to Christ will do so, as Calvin was quick to point out: "Let us remember that although life is promised generally to all who believe in Christ, faith is not common to all. For Christ is open to all and displayed to all, but God opens the eyes only of the elect that they may seek him by faith."[16] For Calvin, John 3:16 spoke not of the extent of God's love, but of the degree and nature of such divine love: God loves the world he has created in spite of its sin, rebellion, and rejection of him. Calvin understood "world" to refer to all of humanity, including the Gentiles, and no longer exclusively to the Israelites of the old covenant.[17] It is to this world that God sends his only begotten Son as Redeemer.[18] Those who interpret "world" to mean every individual person who has ever lived take the phrase differently than Calvin and many other interpreters in the history of the church.[19]

---

[15] Ibid., 74.

[16] Ibid., 75.

[17] Ibid.

[18] Ibid.

[19] See D. A. Carson, *The Gospel according to John*, Pillar New Testament Commentary (Grand Rapids: Eerdmans, 1991), 205: "Jews were familiar with the truth that God loved the children of Israel; here God's love is not restricted by race. Even so, God's love is to be admired not because the world is so big and includes so many people, but because the world is so bad: that is the customary connotation of *kosmos* ('world'). The world is so wicked that John elsewhere forbids Christians to love anything in it (1 Jn. 2:15–17). There

For Calvin, John 3:16 was not an impediment to subscription to the biblical doctrine of election and the simultaneous proclamation of the gospel to all people without exception.

God "Desires All People to Be Saved and to Come to the Knowledge of the Truth"

If John 3:16 is the most popular "anti-Calvinism" passage, 1 Timothy 2:4 may rank as a close second. In his 2001 book *Chosen but Free: A Balanced View of Divine Election*, Christian apologist Norman Geisler attempted to reconcile the biblical tension between the doctrine of election and the Arminian view of libertarian free will. In it he argued, "From the time of the later Augustine this text has been manhandled by extreme Calvinists."[20] He accuses the eminent Puritan exegete John Owen (1616–1683) of holding a typical but "dubious view" in which "all here does not mean all. His tactic is to divert the issue to other passages where 'all' does not mean the whole human race."[21]

It is noteworthy that Owen followed Calvin in his interpretation of this text. For Calvin, the immediate context of 1 Timothy 2:1 helped determine to whom Paul is referring in verse 4 when he writes of God's willing "all people to be saved." Paul is speaking not of every single person in history without exception, but of all types of people, including "kings and those in high positions." So of whom is Paul speaking in verse 4? Like Owen after him, Calvin said that "the present discourse relates to classes of men, and not to individual persons; for his sole object is, to include in this number princes and foreign nations."[22] In a sermon on 1 Timothy 2:3–5, Calvin told his congregation that "St. Paul's meaning is, not that God will save every man, but that the promises which were given to but one people, are now extended to the whole world," meaning,

is no contradiction between this prohibition and the fact that God does love it. Christians are not to love the world with the selfish love of participation; God loves the world with the selfless, costly love of redemption."

[20] Norman L. Geisler, *Chosen but Free: A Balanced View of Divine Election* (Minneapolis: Bethany House, 2001), 201. Geisler refers to those who hold to all five points of the Canons of Dort as "extreme Calvinists."

[21] Ibid., 202.

[22] John Calvin, *Commentaries on the Epistles to Timothy, Titus, and Philemon*, trans. William Pringle (Grand Rapids: Baker, 1996), 54–55.

salvation has come to the entire global community, composed of the Bible's two ethnic categories of people, Jews and Gentiles.[23] While Paul's words here do not mean that God wills the salvation of every single person in world history, still Calvin was certain that the apostle's words are by no means inconsistent with the truth that all who believe will be saved. God will save all kinds of people, whether royalty or commoners, and he will bring to himself people from every nation and ethnicity on earth:

> We must not restrain his fatherly goodness to ourselves alone, nor to any certain number of people. . . . For he showeth that he will be favourable to all. . . .
>
> The gospel is called the mighty power of God, and salvation is to all them that believe: yea, it is a gate of paradise. It follows then, if through the will of God the gospel be preached to all the world, there is a token that salvation is common to all.[24]

Like the Bible, Calvin in his theological writings, commentaries, and sermons was comfortable using the language of universality regarding the necessity of proclaiming the gospel worldwide to all people without distinction.

But where does all this leave the evangelist and missionary? Calvin saw no contradiction between 1 Timothy 2:4 and a full and free offer of the gospel. The command of God is for all human beings everywhere to repent and be reconciled to God, and thus the limiting of "all people" in 1 Timothy 2:4 does nothing to undermine the necessity of preaching the gospel "promiscuously." As Calvin argued:

> But I say nothing on that subject, because it has nothing to do with this passage; for the Apostle simply means, that there is no people and no rank in the world that is excluded from salvation; because God wishes that the gospel should be proclaimed to all without exception. Now the preaching of the gospel gives

[23] John Calvin, *Selected Sermons from the Pastoral Epistles* (Birmingham, AL: Solid Ground, 2012), 97.
[24] Ibid., 98.

life; and hence he justly concludes that God invites all equally to partake of salvation.[25]

Calvin anticipated the challenge that 1 Timothy 2:4 appears to hold for his view of predestination and dealt with the argument that the text renders impossible his view of God's eternal decrees. Paul is addressing all classes of humans and not persons as individuals, he asserted:

> Hence we see the childish folly of those who represent this passage to be opposed to predestination. "If God," they say, "wishes all men indiscriminately to be saved, it is false that some are predestinated by his eternal purpose to salvation, and others to perdition." They might have had some ground for saying this, if Paul were speaking here about individual men; although even then we should not have wanted [i.e., lacked] the means of replying to their argument; for, although the will of God ought not to be judged from his secret decrees, when he reveals them to us by outward signs, yet it does not therefore follow that he has not determined with himself what he intends to do as to every individual man.[26]

In other words, Calvin seems to intimate that the one proclaiming the gospel must see every individual person as potentially "savable," while leaving the secret things of God's decrees to God himself, as Moses admonished the Hebrews in Deuteronomy 29:29, "The secret things belong to the LORD."

"The Lord Is . . . Not Wishing That Any Should Perish, but That All Should Reach Repentance"

In his response to Geisler's attempt at a *via media* between Calvin and Arminius on the nature of the will, James R. White correctly surmised that 2 Peter 3:9, perhaps above all others, is the verse the opponents of Calvin's theology of sovereign grace most often use to

---

[25] Ibid.
[26] Calvin, *Commentaries on the Epistles to Timothy, Titus, and Philemon*, 54.

disprove it: "This is surely the most popular passage cited (almost never with any reference to the context) to 'prove' that God could not possibly desire to save a specific people but instead desires to save every single individual person, thereby denying election and predestination."[27]

The context of the passage is not salvation, but the second coming of Christ and the terrible day of final judgment. As Calvin pointed out in his commentary on 2 Peter, the context and audience are key to a proper interpretation of this disputed verse. Throughout 2 Peter the apostle refers to his intended audience, which, according to the opening verse in chapter 1, is "those who have obtained a faith of equal standing with ours by the righteousness of our God and Savior Jesus Christ." Thus, the intended audience is those who have or would come to salvation through Christ. It is noteworthy that Calvin did not blunt the force of 2 Peter 3:9 for the purpose of evangelizing the lost. Despite the focus of some on the seeming contradiction between Peter's words here and the doctrine of election, this passage, Calvin argued, actually calls all people without exception to repentance and faith in Christ:

> [Peter] checks extreme and unreasonable haste [for the day of resurrection] by . . . [saying that] the Lord defers his coming, that he might invite all mankind to repentance. . . . There is no reason why we should any longer complain of tardiness [in God] . . . who in the best manner regulates time to promote our salvation. And as to the duration of the whole world, we must think exactly the same as of the life of every individual; for God by prolonging time to each, sustains him that he may repent. . . . He does not hasten the end of the world, in order to give to all time to repent.
>
> This is a very necessary admonition, so that we may learn to employ time aright, as we shall otherwise suffer a just punishment for our idleness.

---

[27] James R. White, *The Potter's Freedom: A Defense of the Reformation and a Rebuttal of Norman Geisler's "Chosen but Free"* (Amityville, NY: Calvary, 2000), 145.

... So wonderful is his love toward mankind, that he would have them all to be saved, and is of his own self prepared to bestow salvation on the lost. .... God is ready to receive all to repentance, so that none may perish. .... Every one of us, therefore, who is desirous of salvation, must learn to enter in by this way.[28]

In his comments on this passage, Calvin raised the issue that has cloaked 2 Peter 3:9 in controversy and provided an answer that may surprise many who erroneously believe Calvin to have been an opponent of evangelism and missions:

It may be asked, if God wishes none to perish, why is it so many do perish? To this my answer is, that no mention is here made of the hidden purpose of God, according to which the reprobate are doomed to their own ruin, but only of his will as made known to us in the gospel. For God stretches forth his hand without a difference to all, but lays hold only of those, to lead them to himself, whom he has chosen before the foundation of the world.[29]

Calvin's comments brought to the fore an issue that has been much debated within the church since the advent of the Reformation: Does God, in the Bible, engage in double-talk when he makes it clear in some places (such as 2 Peter 3:9) that he desires every person in human history to be saved, but says in others, such as Ephesians 1, that he chooses all who will be saved before the foundation of the world? In other words, are there "two wills" in God? How did Calvin deal with this biblical tension? The context of 2 Peter 3:9 is an excellent location from which to examine Calvin's take on this knotty question before examining other "universal" texts.

Calvin and the "Two Wills" of God

A crucial piece of the puzzle that provides a full picture, and thus full understanding, of Calvin's soteriology is the Bible's

[28] John Calvin, *Commentaries on the Catholic Epistles*, trans. and ed. John Owen (Grand Rapids: Baker, 1996), 419.
[29] Ibid., 419–20.

two-dimensional depiction of the will of God, the so-called "two wills of God."[30] This doctrine is key to understanding how the Bible can affirm in texts such as Ezekiel 13:23, 33:11, 1 Timothy 2:4, and 2 Peter 3:9 that God desires the salvation of all people, while at the same time the Bible expresses in unambiguous terms God's particular love in electing and predestining those whom "he chose . . . in him before the foundation of the world" (Eph. 1:4). Does God choose or do we choose? Does God want all people saved or not?

The theology of the magisterial Reformers, including Calvin, answered yes to both questions! This doctrine helps us understand the biblical complementarity between the general call of the gospel and predestination, as Calvin expressed it. Contemporary Bible scholar John Piper defines the doctrine this way: "[Scripture teaches] the simultaneous existence of God's will for 'all to be saved' (1 Tim. 2:4) and his will to elect unconditionally those who will actually be saved."[31] This doctrine is fully biblical and is by no means a sign of "divine schizophrenia or exegetical confusion," argues Piper; it "does not contradict biblical expressions of God's compassion for all people, and does not nullify the sincere offers of salvation to everyone who is lost among all the peoples of the world."[32] Calvin, following his theological father, Augustine (354–430), would have agreed. Calvin did not invent the doctrine of the "two wills" of God. In his debate with Dutch Roman Catholic theologian Albert Pighius in *Concerning the Eternal Predestination of God*, and in the *Institutes* and other works, Calvin quotes from Augustine's *Enchiridion* in defense of the doctrine. Moreover, the "two wills" of God is standard teaching in the historic Reformed tradition following the Protestant Reformation.

This issue rose to primacy for Calvin in his somewhat protracted

---

[30] On Calvin's teaching on the two wills, see also Richard A. Muller, "A Tale of Two Wills? Calvin, Amyraut, and Du Moulin on Ezekiel 18:23," in *Calvin and the Reformed Tradition: On the Work of Christ and the Order of Salvation* (Grand Rapids: Baker, 2012), 107–25.

[31] John Piper, "Are There Two Wills in God?," in *Still Sovereign: Contemporary Perspectives on Election, Foreknowledge, and Grace*, ed. Thomas R. Schreiner and Bruce A. Ware (Grand Rapids: Baker, 2000), 107.

[32] Ibid.

debate over predestination with Pighius.[33] Pighius was a key defender of medieval Roman Catholic doctrines during the Reformation, preparing a memorandum, for example, on the divorce of
Henry VIII and also articulating a defense of papal infallibility.
His defense of the freedom of the will, *On the Free Choice of Man
and Divine Grace* (1542), contained an attack on Calvin. In the Reformer's response to Pighius, published at Geneva in 1552, a decade
after Pighius's death, Calvin upbraided his opponent for failing to
understand both the conditionality of the promises of salvation and
the two aspects of God's will. While God wills all to be saved in one
sense and not in another, Calvin assured Pighius that God demands
repentance and faith from all individuals, and that everyone who
calls on the name of the Lord will be saved:

> So again with the promises which invite all men to salvation.
> They do not simply and positively declare what God has de-
> creed in his secret counsel but what he is prepared to do for all
> who are brought to faith and repentance. But, it is alleged, we
> thereby ascribe a double will to God, whereas he is not variable
> and not the least shadow of turning falls upon him. What is this,
> says Pighius, but to mock men, if God professes to will what he
> does not will? But if in fairness the two are read together: I will
> that the sinner turn and live, the calumny is dissolved without
> bother. God demands conversion from us; wherever he finds
> it, a man is not disappointed of the promised reward of life.
> Hence, God is said to will life, as also repentance. But the latter
> he wills, because he invites all to it by his word. Now this is not
> contradictory of his secret counsel, by which he determined to
> convert none but his elect. He cannot rightly on this account be
> thought variable, because as lawgiver he illuminates all with the
> external doctrine of life, in this first sense calling all men to life.
> But in the other sense, he brings to life whom he will, as Father
> regenerating by the Spirit only his sons.[34]

[33] For Calvin's debate with Pighius, see André Pinard, "La notion de grâce irrésistible dans la *Response aux
calomnies d'Albert Pighius* de Jean Calvin" (PhD thesis, University of Laval, 2006).
[34] John Calvin, *Concerning the Eternal Predestination of God*, trans. J. K. S. Reid (Louisville, KY: Westminster
John Knox, 1997), 106, capitalization modernized.

Calvin went on to warn Pighius against putting God in the dock on matters that the finite human mind is not able to grasp fully. Since the identity of the elect is privy to God alone, ministers are obligated to obey the command to preach the Word:

> But why some profit and others do not, far be it from us to say that it is the judgment of the clay and not the potter. . . . Since we do not know who belongs to the number of the predestined and who does not, it befits us to feel as to wish that all be saved. So it will come about that, whoever we come across, we shall study to make him a sharer of peace.[35]

Calvin and the Reformation reasserted the principle of *sola Scriptura*—the Bible alone as the sole authority for the life of faith and doctrine for Christians. Thus, in the *Institutes*, in his sermons, and in his theological writings such as the debate with Pighius, Calvin insisted that he believed in such a complex expression of the will of God for the simple reason that the Bible teaches it. Calvin also emphasized this point in his debate with the Frenchman Sebastian Castellio over God's providence. Castellio had been a colleague of Calvin until a difference of opinion over the canonicity of the Song of Solomon in 1545—Castellio denied it—whereupon Castellio moved to Basel. He later wrote a scathing criticism of Calvin after Geneva executed the anti-Trinitarian Michael Servetus (c. 1511–1553). Castellio drew up fourteen articles in the form of questions, attacking Calvin's theology of predestination and providence. Each of Castellio's questions was framed by ostensibly taking excerpts directly from the writings of Calvin, excerpts which the Reformer rejected as representative of his thought. Calvin felt he had been misquoted and thoroughly misinterpreted by Castel-

---

[35] Ibid., 138. Cf. I. Howard Marshall, "Universal Grace and Atonement in the Pastoral Epistles," in *The Grace of God and the Will of Man*, ed. Clark H. Pinnock (Minneapolis: Bethany House, 1989), 56: "To avoid all misconceptions it should be made clear at the outset that the fact that God wishes or wills that all people should be saved does not necessarily imply that all will respond to the gospel and be saved. We must certainly distinguish between what God would like to see happen and what he actually does will to happen, and both of these things can be spoken of as God's will. The question at issue is not whether all will be saved but whether God has made provision in Christ for the salvation of all, provided that they believe, and without limiting the potential scope of the death of Christ merely to those whom God knows will believe."

lio and responded with a work published in 1558. Calvin accused Castellio of seeking to rationalize God and bring him down to a human level. The absolute providence of God and related doctrines such as election and the "two wills" demonstrate the human inability to fully comprehend the character or ways of God, Calvin argued.

Regarding the "two wills," which Castellio saw as leaving God as the author of sin and evil, Calvin stated:

> If the same apostle with good reason exclaims that his [God's] ways are inscrutable (Rom. 11:33), why am I not allowed to marvel at his secret will even though it is concealed from us? In the book of Job there are many splendid eulogies that celebrate the wisdom of God so that mere mortals may learn not to measure God's wisdom by their own understanding. . . . Will you reproach David for the same foolish reports about God's judgments, when he acknowledged them to be a deep abyss? (Ps. 36:7). From every prophet and apostle I hear the same thing: that the counsel of God is incomprehensible. I embrace by faith without reserve what they declare and what I believe and confidently declare.[36]

Do Calvin's "two wills" saddle God with a self-contradiction as Castellio and some modern-day evangelicals have argued? Contemporary Reformed theologian Wayne Grudem helps us answer the conundrum in a Calvinesque manner:

> Even in the realm of human experience, we know that we can and will carry out something that is painful and that we do not desire (such as punishing a disobedient child or getting an inoculation that temporarily makes us ill) in order to bring about a long-term result that we desire more than the avoidance of short-term pain (to bring about the obedience of a child, for example, or to prevent us from getting a more serious illness). And God is infinitely greater and wiser than we are. Certainly

---

[36] John Calvin, *The Secret Providence of God*, ed. Paul Helm, trans. Keith Goad (Wheaton, IL: Crossway, 2010), 96–97.

it is possible for him to will that his creatures do something that in the short term displeases him in order that in the long term he would receive the greater glory. To say that this is a "self-contradiction" in God is to fail to understand the distinctions that have been made so that this explanation is not contradictory.[37]

In the end, Calvin said we must understand the vast chasm that separates our understanding of how God's will should operate and how God understands himself. Again referencing Augustine approvingly, Calvin wrote: "There is a great difference between what is fitting for man to will and what is fitting for God. . . . For through the bad wills of evil men God fulfills what he righteously wills."[38]

In his lengthy exposition of the doctrine of election in the *Institutes*, Calvin anticipated objections to his expression of the doctrine, objections that placed God's decrees at odds with the free and full call of the gospel. The apostle Paul is a model, Calvin argued, for holding on to a full articulation of God's electing, predestining grace without letting go of the continuing validity of the Great Commission. Paul, after all, was a committed church planter and preached the gospel fully and freely during his missionary travels, and the critics of election would be hard-pressed to match Paul's zeal to see wicked hearts transformed by grace: "What a plain and outspoken preacher of free election Paul was. . . . Was he therefore cold in admonition and exhortation? Let these good zealots compare their earnestness with his: theirs will be found ice compared with his intense fervor."[39]

Paul, he says, sees no such contradiction:

Those moderately versed in Paul will, without long proof, understand how aptly he harmonizes those things which they pretend disagree. Christ commands us to believe in him. Yet when he says, "No one can come to me unless it is granted him

---

[37] Wayne Grudem, *Systematic Theology: An Introduction to Biblical Doctrine* (Grand Rapids: Zondervan, 1994), 332.
[38] Calvin, *Institutes*, 1:234 (1.18.3).
[39] Ibid., 2:961 (3.23.13).

by my Father," [John 6:65], his statement is neither false nor contrary to his command.[40]

Calvin thus held firmly to the doctrine of predestination with one hand while clinging to the continuing validity of the Great Commission in the other. He did so because the Bible seems to do the same.

"Come to Me, All Who Labor and Are Heavy Laden"

Calvin saw Christ's call to sinners for salvation as being universal. There was nothing in his theology that stood as a barrier to the free offer of the gospel, as he makes plain in his comments on Matthew 11:28–30 ("Come to me, all who labor and are heavy laden, and I will give you rest. Take my yoke upon you, and learn from me, for I am gentle and lowly in heart, and you will find rest for your souls. For my yoke is easy, and my burden is light"): "We must attend to the universality of the expression; for Christ included all, without exception, who labor and are burdened, that no man may shut the gate against himself by wicked doubts."[41] While Calvin believed that relatively few among those whom Christ invites to salvation will be converted, nevertheless the free offer of the gospel brings "the relief which he promises" through "the free pardon of sins, which alone give us peace."[42]

The Teaching of Ephesians 1

In a sermon series on Ephesians 1:4–6 that Calvin preached in his exposition of this Pauline letter in 1558 and 1559, the Genevan theologian's doctrine of predestination takes a decidedly more pastoral tone as he sets forth in bold relief both God's absolute choice of his elect and the duty of every person to follow after the one true God. In the third sermon, Calvin especially dealt with the existential question that arises from anxious souls pondering the doctrines of predestination and election for perhaps the first time: What if

---

[40] Ibid.
[41] John Calvin, *Commentary on a Harmony of the Evangelists, Matthew, Mark and Luke*, trans. William Pringle, vol. 2 (Grand Rapids: Baker, 1996), 44.
[42] Ibid.

I am not elect? In a loving but firm pastoral tone, reminiscent of the apostle Paul, Calvin sought to undermine a possible refuge of the unbeliever, asserting boldly that election and predestination provide no excuse for unbelief:

> Many fanciful people say, "Ho! as for me, I shall never know whether God has elected me and, therefore, I must still remain in my perdition." Yes, but that is for want of coming to Jesus Christ. How do we know that God has elected us before the creation of the world? By believing in Jesus Christ. I said before that faith proceeds from election and is the fruit of it, which shows that the root is hidden within.[43]

Faith is the title deed that God's elect receive to show that they were chosen and owned by God before the salvation of the world, a truth that does not override the responsibility of everyone to repent and follow Jesus.

Many charge Calvin with disbelieving "Whosoever will!" But look at the words he spoke his congregation in this sermon:

> Whosoever then believes is thereby assured that God has worked in him, and faith is, as it were, the duplicate copy that God gives us of the original of our adoption. God has his eternal counsel, and he always reserves to himself the chief and original record of which he gives us a copy by faith.[44]

Predestination is the theological caboose and not the engine that pulls salvation along the tracks of God's grace, Calvin argued in essence, and is a doctrine for the spiritually mature; it is not to be presented up front to babes who lack understanding. God has revealed this doctrine not to make souls anxious, but to drive them to their knees in humble worship because, as Calvin averred, God owes no one salvation, only wrath for rejecting the Creator. Ephesians 1, which espouses one of the Bible's most debated doctrines, should not promote further speculation into the

---

[43] John Calvin, *John Calvin's Sermons on Ephesians* (Carlisle, PA: Banner of Truth, 1998), 47.
[44] Ibid.

purposes of God, Calvin said, but should induce humility in the believer.[45]

> The doctrine of predestination does not serve to carry us away into extravagant speculations, but to beat down all pride in us and the foolish opinion we always conceive of our own worthiness and deserts and to show that God has such free power, privilege and sovereign domain over us that he may reprobate whom he pleases and elect whom he pleases; and thus, by this means, we are led to glorify him and further to acknowledge that it is in Jesus Christ he has elected us in order that we should be held fast under the faith of his gospel.[46]

The "Predestination of God Is Indeed . . . a Labyrinth"

In his exposition of Romans 9, Calvin admitted that the "predestination of God is indeed in reality a labyrinth, from which the mind of man can by no means extricate itself."[47] But the tendency of fallen minds is to seek to solve all mysteries pertaining to God, as Calvin wrote:

> So unreasonable is the curiosity of man, that the more perilous the examination of a subject is, the more boldly he proceeds; so that when predestination is discussed, as he cannot restrain himself within due limits, he immediately, through his rashness, plunges himself, as it were, into the depth of the sea.[48]

Paul anticipates this reality in Romans 9, Calvin said, and seeks to deal with objections to God's secret election of individuals to salvation by showing that God is depicted as simultaneously hardening Pharaoh's heart and inviting all people to repent and believe the gospel. That we are unable to reconcile these truths, Calvin believed, owes to our fallen inability to fully understand God's Word and not to a contradiction found in it.

---

[45] Ibid., 48.
[46] Ibid.
[47] John Calvin, *Commentaries on the Epistle of Paul to the Romans*, trans. and ed. John Owen (Grand Rapids: Baker, 1996), 353.
[48] Ibid., 353–54.

"As Many as Were Appointed to Eternal Life Believed"

A key text for the Calvinist tradition has been Acts 13:48, "And when the Gentiles heard this, they began rejoicing and glorifying the word of the Lord, and as many as were appointed to eternal life believed." Indeed, there is little ambiguity in the phrasing, and few other conclusions can be drawn from the grammatical construction than the priority of ordaining before believing; those who believe in Christ have been chosen or ordained unto eternal life by God in the secret counsel of his will before time began. This is precisely Calvin's interpretation in his commentary on the passage.

> For it is a ridiculous cavil to refer this unto the affection of those which believed, as if those received the gospel whose minds were well-disposed. . . . Neither does Luke say that they were ordained unto faith, but unto life; because the Lord predestinates those who are his unto the inheritance of eternal life.[49]

The text, Calvin asserted in no uncertain terms, roots saving faith in election. Nevertheless, as he did in many other places in his works, Calvin warned the unrepentant not to blame their rejection of God on the fact that they may not be chosen; election is no alibi for unbelief, he argued.[50] From a human perspective, salvation comes not to those who are elect, but to those who trust in Christ. Thus, the lost must not worry over whether they are elect or not, but rather, they should flee at once to Christ. As Calvin said:

> Again, because many entangle themselves in doubtful and thorny imaginations, while . . . they seek for their salvation in the hidden counsel of God, let us learn that the election of God is therefore approved by faith, that our minds may be turned unto Christ, as unto the pledge of election, and that they may seek no other certainty save that which is revealed to us in the

---

[49] John Calvin, *Commentary upon the Acts of the Apostles*, trans. Henry Beveridge, vol. 1 (Grand Rapids: Baker, 1996), 555, modernized.
[50] Ibid., 1:557.

gospel; I say, let this seal suffice us, that "whosoever believes
in the only-begotten Son of God has eternal life" [John 3:36].[51]

Hardly the words of one with no apparent concern for those who
stand outside of God's grace.

"For We Know, Brothers Loved by God, That He Has Chosen You"

Some have accused Calvin of looking for signs of regeneration before calling on sinners to repent and believe in Christ. The English
hyper-Calvinist movement of the eighteenth century that left Calvinistic Baptist and Congregationalist churches in a deep freeze
preached this message. Hyper-Calvinist preachers tended to emphasize God's secret will ("Who is among the elect?") to the det-
riment of God's revealed will (the free offer of grace). Fearful of
calling on the reprobate to do something that they lacked the ability to do, hyper-Calvinist ministers refused to invite sinners to flee
to the cross of Christ for rescue.

Some of Calvin's more theologically naive critics have accused
the Reformer of holding the same error. Calvin, however, repeat-
edly warned against seeking to "look behind the veil" of God's
counsel with regard to the doctrine of election. In 1 Thessalonians
1:4–5 ("For we know, brothers loved by God, that he has chosen
you, because our gospel came to you not only in word, but also
in power and in the Holy Spirit and with full conviction"), Calvin made clear that a Christian's knowledge of his own election
comes only after repentance from sin and faith in Christ have been
exhibited.

Thus, from the side of humanity's experiential perspective, election is akin to the caboose of soteriology and not its engine. Commenting on 1 Thessalonians 1:4–5, Calvin warned:

It is to be observed . . . that the election of God, which is in itself hid, is manifested by its marks [i.e., repentance and faith]—

---

[51] Ibid., modernized.

when he gathers to himself the lost sheep and joins them to his flock, and holds out his hand to those that were wandering and estranged from him. Hence a knowledge of our election must be sought from this source.[52]

Still, faith flows from God's secret election, and since it is a doctrine revealed in Scripture, it must not be rejected: "As, however, the secret counsel of God is a labyrinth to those who disregard his calling, so those act perversely who, under the pretext of faith and calling, darken this first grace, from which faith itself flows."[53] Election comes first in God's gracious interaction with his human creatures and manifests itself in faith and effectual calling, Calvin argued, but the reality of election is known only by its fruit in a given Christian. Thus, Calvin made clear throughout all his written works and sermons that the outward call of salvation should be extended to every person within earshot of the proclamation of the Bible.

---

[52] John Calvin, *Commentaries on the Epistles of Paul the Apostle to the Philippians, Colossians, and Thessalonians*, trans. and ed. John Pringle (Grand Rapids: Baker, 1996), 241.
[53] Ibid.

2

"A Sacrifice Well Pleasing to God"

THE DYNAMICS OF JOHN CALVIN'S THEOLOGY OF MISSION

The Victorious Advance of Christ's Kingdom

A frequent theme in Calvin's writings and sermons is that of the victorious advance of Christ's kingdom in the world.[1] God the Father, Calvin declared to Francis I in the prefatory address of his theological masterpiece, the *Institutes of the Christian Religion*, has appointed Christ to "rule from sea to sea, and from the rivers even to the ends of the earth."[2] In a sermon on 1 Timothy 2:5–6, Calvin noted that Jesus came, not simply to save a few, but "to extend his grace over all the world." Similarly, Calvin stated in a sermon on Acts 2 that the reason for the Spirit's descent at Pentecost was that the gospel "reach all the ends and extremities of the world." It was this global perspective on the significance of the gospel that gave Calvin's theology a genuine dynamism and forward movement.

---

[1] Andrew Buckler, *Jean Calvin et la mission de l'Eglise* (Lyon: Editions Olivétan, 2008), 75–86, 115–17.
[2] For this quote and the next two, see David B. Calhoun, "John Calvin: Missionary Hero or Missionary Failure?," *Presbyterion* 5, no. 1 (Spring 1979): 17.

It has been said that if it had not been for the so-called Calvinist wing of the Reformation, many of the great gains of that era
would have died on the vine. While this may be an exaggeration
to some degree, it does illustrate the importance of the Reformed
perspective.[3]

Calvin, moreover, was not satisfied to be involved in simply
reforming the church. He was tireless in seeking to make the influence of the church felt in the affairs of the surrounding society and
thus make God's rule a reality in that area of human life as well.
It was this conviction that led Calvin to be critical of the Anabaptists, the radical left wing of the Reformation. From his perspective, the Anabaptist creation of communities totally separate from
the surrounding culture was really a misguided attempt to flee the
world. Their spiritual forbears were medieval monks, not the early
Christians who had been obedient to Christ's words in Matthew
28:19–20. In Calvin's view, the Anabaptists should have been seeking positive ways in which they could be used by the indwelling
Spirit to impact society in general and reform it, and so advance
the kingdom of Christ.

Means for the Extension of Christ's Kingdom

Calvin was quite certain that the extension of Christ's kingdom is
first of all God's work.[4] Commenting on Matthew 24:30, he asserted
that it is not "by human means but by heavenly power . . . that the
Lord will gather His Church."[5] Or consider his comments on the
phrase "a door was opened for me" in 2 Corinthians 2:12:

> [The meaning of this metaphor is] that an opportunity of fur-
> thering the gospel had presented itself. Just as an open door
> makes an entrance possible, so the Lord's servants make prog-
> ress when opportunity is given them. The door is shut when

---

[3] Jean-Marc Berthoud, "John Calvin and the Spread of the Gospel in France," in *Fulfilling the Great Commission*, Westminster Conference Papers (London: Westminster Conference, 1992), 44–46.
[4] Michael Parsons, *Calvin's Preaching on the Prophet Micah: The 1550–1551 Sermons in Geneva* (Lewiston,
NY: Edwin Mellen, 2006), 205.
[5] Quoted in Calhoun, "John Calvin," 18.

there is no hope of success. Thus when the door is shut we have to go a different way rather than wear ourselves out in vain efforts to get through it but, when an opportunity for edification presents itself, we should realize that a door has been opened for us by the hand of God in order that we may introduce Christ into that place, and we should not refuse to accept the generous invitation that God thus gives us.[6]

For Calvin, the metaphor of an "open door" spoke volumes about the way in which the advance of the church is utterly dependent on the mercy of a sovereign God.[7]

Now, this does not mean that Christians are to be passive in their efforts to reach the lost and can sit back and wait for God to do all. In his comments on Isaiah 12:5 Calvin dealt with this common misinterpretation of God's divine sovereignty:

[Isaiah] shows that it is our duty to proclaim the goodness of God to every nation. While we exhort and encourage others, we must not at the same time sit down in indolence, but it is proper that we set an example before others; for nothing can be more absurd than to see lazy and slothful men who are exciting other men to praise God.[8]

As David Calhoun rightly observes, "The power to save [souls] rests with God but He displays and unfolds His salvation in our preaching of the gospel."[9] While missions and evangelism are indeed God's work, he delights to use his people as his instruments.

Praying for the Lost

The first major way in which God uses his people for the conversion of others is through prayer—our prayers for the conversion

---

[6] John Calvin, *The Second Epistle of Paul the Apostle to the Corinthians and the Epistles to Timothy, Titus and Philemon*, trans. T. A. Smail (Grand Rapids: Eerdmans, 1964), 32, on 2 Cor. 2:12.

[7] See Buckler, *Jean Calvin et la mission de l'Eglise*, 58–64; Jean-François Zorn, "Did Calvin Foster or Hinder the Missions?," *Exchange* 40 (2011): 180–81.

[8] John Calvin, *Commentary on the Book of the Prophet Isaiah*, trans. William Pringle, vol. 1 (Grand Rapids: Baker, 1996), 403.

[9] Calhoun, "John Calvin," 18.

of unbelievers. Calvin valued prayer deeply. While many modern-day systematic theologies neglect the subject of prayer altogether, Calvin spent one of the longest sections in the entire 1559 edition of his *Institutes* on prayer. His discussion of prayer is found within book 3, on soteriology, "The Way in Which We Receive the Grace of Christ," and is sandwiched between chapter 19, on Christian freedom, and chapter 21, on the doctrines of election and predestination. Prayer obviously occupied an important place in the system of Calvin's theology, for he viewed it as a grace central to the Christian faith and closely tied to the salvation of God's elect. We see this conviction about prayer at work in Calvin's own prayers, a good number of which have been recorded for us at the end of his sermons. Each of his sermons on Deuteronomy, for instance, ends with a prayer that runs something like this: "May it please him [i.e., God] to grant this [saving] grace, not only to us, but also to all peoples and nations of the earth."[10]

Elsie McKee correctly argues that Calvin saw 1 Timothy 2:1–2, a passage examined in the previous chapter, as providing biblical warrant for praying for "all people who dwell on earth," including those who walk on a path of darkness, that Christ might bring them into his city of light.[11] The Lord's Prayer, sometimes called the model prayer, given by the Lord Jesus in the Sermon on the Mount, also informed Calvin's prayer for the nations, particularly the second petition, in which Jesus taught his disciples to pray to the Father, "Your kingdom come." In the final edition of the *Institutes*, Calvin developed in great detail the implications of each of the six petitions of the Lord's Prayer. In praying "Your kingdom come," Calvin surmised that, in part, we are asking God to spread his kingdom across the world. From the first edition of the *Institutes* in 1536 to the final edition in 1559, there is a shift in emphasis in Calvin's theological exposition of this phrase from individual obedience to the planting of churches: "We must daily desire that

---

[10] Ibid., 19n23.
[11] Elsie McKee, "Calvin and Praying for 'All People Who Dwell on Earth,'" *Interpretation* 63, no. 2 (April 2009): 130.

God gather churches unto himself from all parts of the earth," Calvin maintained.[12]

But if God knows everything, why pray? The answer is that much as preaching serves as God's chosen means to enlighten, convict, and draw the unconverted, Calvin viewed prayer as another means by which God applies grace in the redemption of those outside his salvific grace. Prayer does not so much change God, but it is a factor that God has ordained to be a part of the salvation of his elect people. Bruce A. Ware summarizes Calvin's view well:

> It was surely Calvin's perspective that prayer . . . does make a difference to the work of God. While prayer never coerces God to act other than his infinite wisdom has willed, it nevertheless is one important and necessary condition which must be present for certain aspects of God's work to be carried out. Prayer, then, is not contrary to divine sovereignty but a divinely ordained instrument functioning within the sphere of God's sovereign wisdom and power in carrying out his will.[13]

In answering the crucial concern about the purpose of prayer, Calvin opened his section on prayer in the final edition of the *Institutes* with a handful of reasons why prayer is necessary. God is sovereign and rules in his providence over all people and events, yet God's people mysteriously but actually participate in divine activity through prayer, Calvin argued; and thus a Christian must never use God's sovereign kingship as an excuse for idleness in constant prayer:

> Therefore they act with excessive foolishness who, to call men's minds away from prayer, babble that God's providence, standing guard over all things, is vainly importuned with our entreaties, inasmuch as the Lord has not, on the contrary, vainly

---

[12] David B. Calhoun, "Prayer: The Chief Exercise of Faith," in *Theological Guide to Calvin's Institutes: Essays and Analysis*, ed. David W. Hall and Peter A. Lillback (Phillipsburg, NJ: P&R, 2008), 362. The quote is from John Calvin, *Institutes of the Christian Religion*, ed. John T. McNeill, trans. Ford Lewis Battles (Philadelphia: Westminster Press, 1960), 2:905 (3.20.42).

[13] Bruce A. Ware, "The Role of Prayer and the Word in the Christian Life according to John Calvin," *Studia Biblica et Theologica* 12 (1982): 90.

attested that "he is near . . . to all who call upon his name in truth" [Ps. 145:19].[14]

Moreover, Calvin admonished believers not to be discouraged if they do not see fruit immediately issuing as a result of their prayers. As he stated in his comments on Genesis 17:23:

> So, at this day, God seems to enjoin a thing impossible to be done, when he requires his gospel to be preached everywhere in the whole world, for the purpose of restoring it from death to life. For we see how great is the obstinacy of nearly all men, and what numerous and powerful methods of resistance Satan employs; so that, in short, all the ways of access to these principles are obstructed. Yet it behooves individuals to do their duty, and not to yield to impediments; and, finally, our endeavors and our labors shall by no means fail of that success, which is not yet apparent.[15]

Other Means for Reaching the Lost

Believers must also actively employ their strength to bring God's salvation to others. In his sermon on Deuteronomy 33:18–19, Calvin argued that it is not enough to be involved in God's service. Christians need to be drawing others to serve and adore God.[16] Specifically, how does God use the strength of Christians? Calvin's answer was that it is by their words and by their deeds. Given Calvin's high appreciation of the Word of God, one would naturally expect that this would be seen as a major means of witness. Thus, Calvin observed that whenever the Old Testament prophets foretold "the renewal of the Church or its extension over the whole globe," they always assigned "the first place to the Word."[17] Acting on this conviction, Calvin encouraged the translation and printing

---

[14] Calvin, *Institutes*, 2:853 (3.20.3).

[15] John Calvin, *Commentaries on the First Book of Moses Called Genesis*, trans. John King, vol. 1 (Grand Rapids: Baker, 1996), 465.

[16] Sermon 196, on Deut. 33:18–19, in *Ioannis Calvini Opera quae supersunt omnia*, ed. William Baum, Edward Cunitz, and Edward Reuss, *Corpus Reformatorum* 57 (Brunswick, 1885; repr., New York: Johnson Reprint Corporation, 1964), 29:175.

[17] Quoted in Calhoun, "John Calvin," 22.

of the Scriptures in the work of Reformation in Geneva. This also explains his own devotion to regular expository preaching and his penning of commentaries on all of the books of the New Testament (except for 2 and 3 John and Revelation) and on a goodly number of Old Testament books.

Witness is borne not only by the Word, but also by our deeds. Thus, Calvin established an academy in Geneva to train men to be missionaries for his native land, France.[18] A large number of these men did indeed go back as missionaries, and some died as martyrs. To five such missionaries who had been arrested at Lyons and were facing death by martyrdom, Calvin wrote on May 15, 1553:

> Since it pleases him [i.e., God] to employ you to the death in maintaining his quarrel [with the world], he will strengthen your hands in the fight, and will not suffer a single drop of your blood to be spent in vain. And though the fruit may not all at once appear, yet in time it shall spring up more abundantly than we can express. But as he hath vouchsafed you this privilege, that your bonds have been renowned, and that the noise of them has been everywhere spread abroad, it must needs be, in despite of Satan, that your death should resound far more powerfully, so that the name of our Lord be magnified thereby. For my part, I have no doubt, if it please this kind Father to take you unto himself, that he has preserved you hitherto, in order that your long-continued imprisonment might serve as a preparation for the better awakening of those whom he has determined to edify by your end. For let enemies do their utmost, they never shall be able to bury out of sight that light which God has made to shine in you, in order to be contemplated from afar.[19]

Here Calvin considered the act of martyrdom a powerful witness for the gospel, though it is one without words.

---

[18] See chap. 3.
[19] Letter 318, in *Letters of John Calvin*, ed. Jules Bonnet, trans. David Constable, 2 vols. (1858; repr., New York: Lenox Hill, 1972), 2:406.

Calvin also saw Christians as examples of godliness or piety to their neighbors and believed that this in itself may well draw them to God. In concluding his sermon on Micah 2:4–5, for example, Calvin said:

> In light of the benefit of having God's Word preached with purity to us, let us be willing to conform our lives more and more to his good will, *in order that by doing so the unconverted*, beholding our good life and conduct, *might be drawn to God's understanding*, to the end that God's name be glorified by all, with common accord.[20]

Calvin was also convinced that each and every Christian must be prepared to witness, by both word and deed, about God's grace and mercy in Christ, and to all whom they can. When it came to the spreading of the gospel, it is noteworthy that Calvin made no distinction between the responsibility of pastors and that of other Christians. All believers must be involved.[21] In his concluding section in the *Institutes* on preaching the doctrine of predestination, for instance, Calvin was clear that believers must proclaim the gospel to every person in their path, while knowing that it is God's prerogative to save whom he will; the command to believers is merely to preach the Word. As was his pattern throughout his magnum opus, Calvin quoted Augustine's work *On Rebuke and Grace* in affirming the necessity of universal repentance and faith, as well as the necessity of the universal call of the gospel:

> "For as we do not know who belongs to the number of the predestined or who does not belong, we ought to be so minded as to wish that all men be saved." So shall it come about that we try to make every one we meet a sharer in our peace. But our peace will rest upon the sons of peace . . . [and] a healthful and severe rebuke should be applied as a medicine to all that they may not either perish themselves or destroy others. It belongs

---

[20] Sermon on Mic. 2:4–5 in John Calvin, *Sermons on the Book of Micah*, trans. and ed. Benjamin Wirt Farley (Phillipsburg, NJ: P&R, 2003), 92–93, emphasis added.
[21] Calhoun, "John Calvin," 22; Parsons, *Calvin's Preaching on the Prophet Micah*, 209–11, 224.

to God, however, to make that rebuke useful to those whom he
. . . has foreknown and predestined.[22]

There is one means that Calvin expected God to use in the
spread of the gospel that we today in the West probably do not
expect: evangelism through Christian rulers and magistrates.[23]
For example, when Elizabeth I (1533–1603) came to the throne of
England, Calvin saw it as a hopeful sign for the advance of the gospel in England. Over the years he also corresponded extensively
with a number of French noblewomen, including Jeanne d'Albret
(1528–1572), queen of Navarre, and Renée d'Este (1510–1575), the
Duchess of Ferrara. These French noblewomen played a significant
role in the French Reformation, and Calvin recognized his need of
their support, and that of other nobility, if new territories were to
be opened up to the spread of the evangelical faith.[24] Thus, in his
commentary on 1 Timothy 2:1–2, where Paul encourages prayer for
kings and those in authority, Calvin noted that Christians ought to
"ask God to make wicked rulers good" so that they might "promote
religion, . . . maintain the worship of God and . . . require reverence
for sacred things."[25]

Motivations for Extending Christ's Kingdom

What was to motivate the believer in bearing witness to the faith?
First and foremost was the glory of God. As Calvin stated in his
sermon on Deuteronomy 33:18–19: "When we know God to be our
Father, should we not desire that he be known as such by all? And
if we do not have this passion, that all creatures do him homage, is
it not a sign that his glory means little to us?"[26] In other words, if
we are truly passionate about God's glory, this passion will result

---

[22] Calvin, *Institutes*, 2:964 (3.23.14).
[23] Buckler, *Jean Calvin et la mission de l'Eglise*, 177–98.
[24] See, for example, the following study on Calvin's friendship with Renée d'Este, the Duchess of Ferrara: Peter Y. de Jong, "Calvin and the Duchess of Ferrara (An Inquiry into Calvin's Pastoral Ministry)," *Mid-America Journal of Theology* 1, no. 1 (Spring 1985): 32–86; and Machiel A. van den Berg, *Friends of Calvin*, trans. Reinder Bruinsma (Grand Rapids: Eerdmans, 2009), 48–57. On Renée, see also Simonetta Carr, *Renée de France* (Darlington, UK: EP Books, 2013).
[25] Commentary on 1 Tim. 2:2 in Calvin, *Second Corinthians and the Epistles to Timothy, Titus and Philemon*, 207.
[26] Sermon 196, on Deut. 33:18–19, in *Ioannis Calvini Opera*, 29:175, trans. Michael A. G. Haykin.

in witness. Then we are to evangelize for the simple reason that we have been commanded to do so by Christ.[27]

Moreover, bearing witness to the faith is pleasing to God. Consider in this regard the following extract from a letter Calvin wrote to a Christian landowner on the island of Jersey around the year 1553:

> We praise God for having inclined your heart to try if it will be possible to erect, by your means, a small church on the place where you reside. And indeed, according as the agents of the Devil strive by every act of violence to abolish the true religion, extinguish the doctrine of salvation, and exterminate the name of Jesus Christ, it is very just that we should labor on, our side to further the progress of the gospel, that, by these means, God may be served in purity, and the poor wandering sheep may be put under the protection of the sovereign Pastor to whom everyone should be subject. And you know that it is a sacrifice well pleasing to God, to advance the spread of the Gospel by which we are enlightened in the way of salvation, to dedicate our life to the honor of him who has ransomed us at so costly a price in order to bear rule in the midst of us.[28]

Compassion for the lost condition of people also should drive Christians to witness. "If we have any humanity in us," Calvin declared in a sermon on Deuteronomy 33, "seeing men going to perdition, . . . ought we not be moved by pity, to rescue the poor souls from hell, and teach them the way of salvation?"[29] In fact, a Christian who is not involved in witness is really a contradiction in terms. As Calvin remarked in his commentary on Isaiah 2:3:

> The godly will be filled with such an ardent desire to spread the doctrines of religion, that everyone not satisfied with his own calling and his personal knowledge will desire to draw others along with him. And indeed nothing could be more inconsis-

---

[27] Calhoun, "John Calvin," 20.

[28] Letter 339, in Bonnet, *Letters of John Calvin*, 2:453.

[29] Sermon 196, on Deut. 33:18–19, in *Ioannis Calvini Opera*, 29:175, trans. Michael A. G. Haykin.

tent with the nature of faith than that deadness which would lead a man to disregard his brethren, and to keep the light of knowledge choked up within his own breast.[30]

Again, in his commentary on 1 Timothy 2, Calvin cited love toward neighbor as the compelling impetus for Christians to pray for all people to know God and thus be saved:

> Since the preaching of the Gospel brings life, [Paul] rightly concludes that God regards all [people] as being equally worthy to share in salvation. . . . There is a duty of love to care a great deal for the salvation of all those to whom God extends his call and to testify to this by godly prayers.[31]

A concern for unbelievers permeated Calvin's pastoral prayers as well. McKee quotes a prayer Calvin prepared for his liturgy, "The Form of Prayers." In it, his pastoral, prayerful concern for the lost rings loud and clear:

> We pray you now, O most gracious God and merciful Father, for all people everywhere. As it is your will to be acknowledged as the Savior of the whole world, through the redemption wrought by your Son Jesus Christ, grant that those who are still estranged from the knowledge of him, being in the darkness and captivity of error and ignorance, may be brought by the illumination of your Holy Spirit and the preaching of your gospel to the right way of salvation, which is to know you, the only true God, and Jesus Christ whom you have sent (John 17:3).[32]

Calvin's own prayers, like this one for the extension of the gospel to "all people everywhere" and to "the whole world," illustrate the truth of Andrew Buckler's observation that, for Calvin, prayer is the first thing we must do in mission.[33]

---

[30] Calvin, *Commentary on the Book of the Prophet Isaiah*, 1:94.

[31] Calvin, *Second Corinthians and the Epistles to Timothy, Titus and Philemon*, 209, on 1 Tim. 2:3.

[32] Quoted in McKee, "Calvin and Praying for 'All People,'" 139.

[33] Buckler, *Jean Calvin et la mission de l'Eglise*, 207.

3

"How Very Important This Corner Is"

THE CALVINISTIC MISSIONS TO FRANCE AND BRAZIL

Geneva as a Missionary Center

Geneva was not a large city. Nevertheless, it became *the* missionary center of Europe during the time of Calvin's ministry, and that largely through the influx of religious refugees. Beginning in 1542, Protestants from numerous regions and countries, including England, Italy, the Netherlands, and Scotland, fled to Geneva in a steady stream. So great was the influx of persecuted Protestants that the population of Geneva doubled by 1555 and reached a peak of slightly more than twenty-one thousand by 1560.[1]

Though this ingathering threatened to overwhelm the available accommodations of Geneva, Calvin was pleased to have so many sympathizers of the Reformation gather in his city.[2] Expressing his

---

[1] Scott L. Simmons, "John Calvin and Missions: A Historical Study," in *Calvin and World Mission: Essays*, ed. Thomas Schirrmacher (Nürnberg: VTR, 2009), 191; Alister E. McGrath, *A Life of John Calvin: A Study in the Shaping of Western Culture* (Oxford: Blackwell, 1990), 121.

[2] Philip E. Hughes makes a compelling point in arguing that those who fled from persecution in France and other places to Geneva would not likely have left one tyrannical set of government leaders to follow

pleasure to his close friend Guillaume Farel (1489–1565) in 1551, Calvin wrote: "I am . . . much preoccupied with the foreigners who daily pass through this place in great numbers, or who come here to live. . . . Should you pay us a visit next autumn, you will find our city considerably increased—a pleasing spectacle to me, if they do not overwhelm me with their visits."[3] In Calvin's view, it was no accident that refugees were flooding to Geneva; such an influx was nothing short of a providential opportunity for the Reformation and its gospel to grow beyond the walls of that city and into the sinful hearts of humans across the continent. Thus, Calvin sought to harness the energies and gifts of many of these refugees so as to make Geneva central to the expansion of Reformation thought and piety throughout Europe. This meant training and preparing many of these refugees to go back to their native lands as evangelists and Reformers. And first and foremost on Calvin's heart as a place needing the gospel was his home and native land, France.

The Mission to France

France in the sixteenth century was a deeply religious nation. What Jean-Marc Berthoud calls "superstitious Romanist piety" blanketed parts of France as a result of a popular revival of religion in the early part of the century, but such piety was a far cry from the core doctrines of the apostles.[4] Henri II (1519–1559), the Roman Catholic king of France, despised the reform movement and was determined to suppress it at every turn. He persecuted the nascent Protestant movement across his kingdom, even as the Huguenots (as the members of the Protestant Reformed church of France came to be called) grew into a significantly large minority during his reign from 1547 to 1559. In June of 1559, Henri was seriously injured in a joust-

---

the leadership of another tyrant if Calvin's critics are correct in their assessment of the Reformer as a man and a theologian. "After all," writes Hughes, "there were other hospitable cities, without a Calvin, whose gates were open to them and where they could be sure of a welcome. But they chose to go to Geneva. And it was Calvin, the so-called 'man-hater,' who was their champion." "John Calvin: Director of Missions," in *The Heritage of John Calvin*, ed. John H. Bratt (Grand Rapids: Eerdmans, 1973), 43–44.

[3] Letter 279, in *Letters of John Calvin*, ed. Jules Bonnet, trans. David Constable, 2 vols. (1858; repr., New York: Lenox Hill, 1972), 2:313, modernized.

[4] Jean-Marc Berthoud, "John Calvin and the Spread of the Gospel in France," in *Fulfilling the Great Commission*, Westminster Conference Papers (London: Westminster Conference, 1992), 4.

ing match. The king died ten days later from a splinter that had penetrated his brain through the eye. The French throne passed to François II (1544–1560), a sickly fifteen-year-old boy who was nothing more than a pathetic marionette to his mother, Catherine de' Medici (1519–1589). François was married to Mary, Queen of Scots (1542–1587), and under his brief reign, efforts to exterminate Protestants intensified markedly. The royal House of Guise and the Cardinal of Lorraine rose to power with François on the throne, and both were determined to bring the curtain down on Protestantism forever.

In 1559 and 1560, arrests among Protestants rose exponentially. Life for Reformed ministers, missionaries, and parishioners darkened significantly in the spring of 1562 with the outbreak of what is known to history as the French Wars of Religion. The powder keg exploded on March 1, 1562, when soldiers of the House of Guise opened fire on five hundred Reformed worshipers at Wassy in northeastern France, killing thirty. Within a month, violence against Protestant Christians exploded across France in a series of massacres. Cathedrals were ransacked and in July, Protestants were declared outlaws who could be killed freely and legally without fear of arrest.[5] It was for this context that Calvin prepared men to proclaim the biblical gospel of the Reformation, and likely even be martyred for it.[6]

Berthoud rightly asks the central question that arises when one seeks to reconcile John Calvin's name and the enterprise of global missions and evangelization:

> How is one to account for the fact that the preaching of such apparently humanly debilitating doctrines as those of predestination, the utter depravity of human beings—which all too many

[5] Bruce Gordon, *Calvin* (New Haven, CT: Yale University Press, 2009), 320–21.

[6] For details of the mission to France, see especially Berthoud, "John Calvin and the Spread of the Gospel," 1–53; Berthoud, *Calvin et la France: Genève et le déploiement de la Réforme au XVIe siècle* (Lausanne: Editions L'Age d'Homme, 1999); Andrew Buckler, *Jean Calvin et la mission de l'Eglise* (Lyon: Editions Olivétan, 2008), 45–47, 133–200; and Jon Balserak, "Examining the Myth of Calvin as a Lover of Order," in *The Myth of the Reformation*, ed. Peter Opitz, Refo500 Academic Studies 9 (Göttingen: Vandenhoeck & Ruprecht, 2013), 160–75.

Evangelical Christians today declare to be counter-productive of effective evangelization—should have in fact produced one of the most spectacular revivals in the history of the Church? For the preaching of the Reformation not only led to the conversion of countless men and women to an extremely demanding faith, but in addition, produc[ed] a thoroughgoing transformation of the cultural, social and political mores of great segments of Western civilization, the likes of which we have not seen since.[7]

In 1555, Geneva began sending ministers to serve in the infant Protestant churches in France.[8] Between 1555 and 1562, it is estimated that nearly a hundred ministers left the safe haven of Geneva and traveled surreptitiously to destinations all over the French kingdom.[9] New churches across France sent desperate appeals to Geneva for an increased flow of ministers, far more than the city could supply.[10] Calvin sought to educate the ministers as best he could, providing them with basic Bible instruction. In his important study of Calvin's Geneva and its ministers, *Geneva and the Coming of the Wars of Religion in France, 1555–1563*, Robert M. Kingdon estimated that about one thousand students attended Calvin's daily lectures.[11] In 1559, Calvin founded the Academy in Geneva under the rectorship of Theodore Beza (1519–1605) for the training of both youth and future ministers of Geneva and points abroad in Europe. As the Protestant churches spread in France, watered by the rain of persecution, the new congregations depended on Geneva at the end of the 1550s to supply ministers.[12]

The effort was successful. It is estimated that by 1559 there were at least fifty-nine churches across the kingdom of France.[13] In 1555, there had been but five Reformed churches in France. Between 1555 and 1562, "just under a hundred ministers left the relative safety

---

[7] Berthoud, "Calvin and the Spread of the Gospel," 2.

[8] Gordon, *Calvin*, 312–13.

[9] Ibid., 313.

[10] Ibid.

[11] Robert M. Kingdon, *Geneva and the Coming of the Wars of Religion in France, 1555–1562* (Geneva: Droz, 1956), 14–15. See also Gordon, *Calvin*, 313.

[12] Gordon, *Calvin*, 300.

[13] Ibid., 306.

of Geneva and the Vaud to face appalling risks; they travelled in clandestine manner to avoid detection, and knew that capture meant torture and death."[14] The church experienced sizable growth during the years 1560 and 1561, with an estimated 20 percent of the population of Rouen, for example, embracing the Christian faith.[15] Calvin was vitally involved in every aspect of this missionary work. He taught the Scriptures to the budding ministers, oversaw their pastoral training in Geneva, as well as in Neuchâtel and the Vaud, examined them, and then presented them for ordination and commissioning to France.[16] The missions-sending efforts peaked in 1561 and 1562 with at least 150 ministers sent out from Geneva to preach the gospel in France.[17] By 1562, the number of Reformed churches was over two thousand, and the total number of members estimated within these churches stood at two million—approximately 10 percent of the entire population of France (twenty million), but comprising close to half of the upper and middle classes.[18]

While the figures available to us are anything but complete, they clearly demonstrate that Calvin was anything but anti-missions and anti-evangelism. The numbers that have been compiled are limited to the years between 1555 and 1562, when it was felt safe enough that the names of the Geneva missionaries might be recorded without putting them in grave danger.[19] The outbreak of wars in France in 1562 demanded that the names of many evangelical ministers and their destinations be concealed for the sake of prudence. Many of the men adopted pseudonyms in carrying out their work. Philip Hughes describes the climate into which these missionaries were deployed:

> It would be hard to exaggerate the extremely hazardous nature of the assignment undertaken by those who sallied forth from

---

[14] Ibid., 312–13.

[15] Ibid., 315.

[16] Ibid.

[17] Kingdon, *Geneva and the Coming of the Wars of Religion*, 79.

[18] Mark Greengrass, *The French Reformation* (Oxford: Blackwell, 1987), 43; Berthoud, "Calvin and the Spread of the Gospel," 25.

[19] Many of the available names have been revealed through Geneva's Register of the Company of Pastors, which is a key source in Kingdon's important work *Geneva and the Coming of the Wars of Religion*.

Geneva as missionaries. The unbridled hostility to the Reformation meant that the utmost secrecy had to be observed in sending out these evangelical emissaries. . . . Their lines of infiltration were along perilous paths through the mountains, where they were dependent on friendly cottagers for food and hiding in case of necessity. Nor did the danger end when they arrived at their various destinations, for there too the utmost caution had to be observed lest they should be discovered and apprehended, with all the dire consequences that would be involved. Where a congregation was mustered, services were conducted in a private home behind locked doors or in the shadows of a woodland hillside. There were times when, as much for the sake of the work as for his own safety, it became advisable for a missionary-pastor to leave a place because his activities were becoming suspect and his identity was no longer well concealed.[20]

Overall, there was much about the mission to France that was a missionary success story, even though the long-term history of these French Calvinist churches is one of deep tragedy.[21] In a letter to the German divine Wenceslaus Zuleger (1530–1596) that Calvin wrote at the close of August 1558, the French Reformer reported as much as he spoke highly of the Protestant churches planted in France and lauded the courage of their pastors—trained in and sent out from Geneva—who labored faithfully in the face of persecution. God was receiving great glory, he said, from their labors on behalf of the gospel.

God protects in a miraculous manner the little churches which are scattered up and down France; nay, amid the atrocious threats of our enemies, he gives an increase which no one would ever have dared to hope. . . . The number of the faithful is everywhere increasing, and already in very many places secret meetings are held.[22]

---

[20] Philip Edgcumbe Hughes, "John Calvin: Director of Missions," in Bratt, *Heritage of John Calvin*, 46.
[21] See the recent account of this history in Geoffrey Treasure, *The Huguenots* (New Haven, CT: Yale University Press, 2013).
[22] John Calvin, *Tracts and Letters*, ed. Jules Bonnet, trans. Marcus Robert Gilchrist, 7 vols. (1858; repr., Edinburgh: Banner of Truth, 2009), 6:463.

The Mission to Brazil

A mission in which Calvin was involved that was not a success was the mission to Brazil. It does, however, serve to illustrate Calvin's global vision for the spread of the gospel and further demolishes the critique of the Reformers in general, and Calvin in particular, that they lacked interest in seeing the gospel spread across the globe.

French sailors had been at the forefront of trading expeditions in the Americas, but were slow to establish a colony. In 1555 an opportunity came to establish a colony on an island off the shore of Brazil in the Bay of Guanabara (Rio de Janeiro).[23] Backing the colony was the prominent Huguenot leader Gaspard de Coligny (1519–1572), the Lord High Admiral of France, and leading the expedition was Nicolas Durand de Villegagnon (1510–1571), who had known Calvin since the early 1530s in Paris. Villegagnon seemed sympathetic to the cause of the Reformation, and now at Coligny's behest sought to establish a French Protestant refuge in the New World. Villegagnon wrote to Calvin and the Genevan church in 1556 asking the Reformer for pastors to accompany the colonists, six hundred or so in number. In his words, he hoped the pastors would be able to "better reform him and his people, and to draw the savages to the knowledge of their salvation."[24] After the other pastors of Geneva had consulted with one another and presumably with Calvin—the Reformer was away from Geneva when the request actually arrived—two pastors were sent, Guillaume Chartier and Pierre Richier, who arrived in Brazil on March 10, 1557, along with a dozen or so other Swiss Calvinists, all personally chosen by Calvin. According to Jean de Léry (1536–1613), a participant on the voyage, the Genevan elders "gave thanks to God for the extension

[23] For what follows, see G. Baez-Camargo, "The Earliest Protestant Missionary Venture in Latin America," *Church History* 21 (1952): 135–45; R. Pierce Beaver, "The Genevan Mission to Brazil," in Bratt, *The Heritage of John Calvin*, 55–73; Amy Glassner Gordon, "The First Protestant Missionary Effort: Why Did It Fail?," *International Bulletin of Missionary Research* 8, no. 1 (January 1984): 12–18; Buckler, *Jean Calvin et la mission de l'Eglise*, 35–41; Jean-François Zorn, "Did Calvin Foster or Hinder the Missions?," *Exchange* 40 (2011): 181–83.

[24] From Jean de Léry, *Histoire d'un voyage fait en la terre de Brésil* (Paris, 1578), quoted in Buckler, *Jean Calvin et la mission de l'Eglise*, 36; and Zorn, "Did Calvin Foster or Hinder the Missions?," 182.

of the reign of Jesus Christ in such a far-off land . . . and among a nation entirely ignorant of the true God."[25]

As it turned out, though, the mission failed. Quarrels soon erupted between the Genevan Protestants and some of the Roman Catholics among the colonists over the nature of the Lord's Supper, which was one of the most hotly contested issues in the sixteenth century, and how to baptize infants. Villegagnon turned against the Protestants and expelled them from the island to the mainland, where they had to wait two months for a ship to take them back to Europe. De Léry was able to make important ethnographic observations of some of the native Brazilians, the Tupinamba, but the Protestants failed to lead any of them to Christ. Villegagnon himself also abandoned the colony, returned to France, and tried to goad Calvin into a public debate about the differences between his theology and that of the Roman Church. Calvin refused to be drawn into public controversy with Villegagnon, though Pierre Richier, one of the Genevan pastors who had been with Villegagnon in Brazil, did pen a bitter *ad hominem* attack on the French sailor.

At the turn of the twentieth century, S. L. Morris speculated about what might have happened if the colony had prospered and some of the Tupinamba people had been won to Christ:

> One can scarcely avoid speculation as to what "might have been," if the unfortunate mission had not been thus prematurely wrecked. As Calvin's name is associated with Augustine, the great theologian, might it not also been linked with Augustine [of Canterbury] the missionary in the conversion of a continent? If the seeds of Protestant Christianity planted by him in South America had germinated, who can say if the glory of that misguided continent might not have shone with all the luster of Protestant North America.[26]

[25] From Léry, *Histoire d'un voyage fait en la terre de Brésil*, quoted in Buckler, *Jean Calvin et la mission de l'Eglise*, 37.

[26] S. L. Morris, "The Relation of Calvin and Calvinism to Mission," in *Calvin Memorial Addresses*, ed. Benjamin B. Warfield et al. (1909; repr., Birmingham, AL: Solid Ground Christian Books, 2007), 130–31.

Notwithstanding the ethnic triumphalism evident in this text, these comments about an alternate history for Latin America make for fascinating speculation. But such was not to be: the mission was short-circuited and did not bear the desired fruit. Nevertheless, it does serve to demonstrate Calvin's missionary spirit and a desire for the conversion of the nations. As Morris wrote, "Alas! His missionary venture served no useful purpose, except to exhibit his Christian spirit and benevolent attitude toward world-wide evangelization in obedience to the Great Commission."[27] Morris argued that the attempt to fulfill the Great Commission in Brazil served as a precursor to the world-mission enterprise that would arrive in the person of William Carey more than two hundred years later.[28] The theology of sovereign grace that Calvin held so dear would be the very theology that undergirded the gospel that Carey and his friends took from England to Serampore.

> Just as a premature blossom in the treacherous Indian summer, though nipped by the early frosts of winter, is nevertheless a prophecy of the coming spring; so Calvin's ill-timed evangelism was but the guarantee of the evangelistic spirit of Calvinism, when the springtime of favorable seasons should furnish opportunity to flower out in the glorious harvest of the world's conversion.[29]

This Brazilian mission and, even more so, the mission to France indicate that Calvin was surely right when he told the Swiss German Reformer Heinrich Bullinger (1504–1575) in 1549 about Geneva and its missionary impact in the world of their day: "When I consider how very important this corner [i.e., Geneva] is for the propagation of the kingdom of Christ, I have good reason to be anxious that it should be carefully watched over."[30]

---

[27] Ibid.
[28] Ibid.
[29] Ibid., 131.
[30] Letter to Heinrich Bullinger, May 7, 1549, in *Tracts and Letters*, ed. Jules Bonnet, trans. Marcus Robert Gilchrist, 7 vols. (1858; repr., Edinburgh: Banner of Truth, 2009), 2:227.

4

"To Convert the World"

THE PURITANS AND BEING MISSIONAL
IN THE SEVENTEENTH CENTURY

Recent Trends in Writing History

For much of the twentieth century, evangelicalism was not a popular subject of scholarly research. Many twentieth-century historians had discounted the importance of religion in history, for deep religiosity was not part of their own experience, and thus evangelicalism, which is first and foremost a religious movement, was beyond the pale of their interest. The maudlin excesses of nineteenth-century Victorian evangelicals also made the exploration of religious sensibility somewhat embarrassing.

But historiographical fashions change, and there is now a very welcome renewal of interest in charting the history of evangelicalism. One of the pioneers in this resurgence is David Bebbington, whose inductive tour de force *Evangelicalism in Modern Britain* (1989) identified an evangelical "quadrilateral of priorities," four distinguishing marks that set evangelicalism apart from other Christian traditions. According to Bebbington's analysis, which begins with the emergence of evangelicalism in the 1730s, evangelicals first "held and practiced the conviction that lives have to be transformed by the gospel, that people are not naturally Christians,"[1] a conviction that Bebbington terms "conversionism." Then, there has been "activism," which consists "primarily in spreading the gospel," that is, evangelism and missionary activity, but which also involves doing "all sorts of humane work of charity."[2] Third, evangelicalism has been marked by what Bebbington calls "biblicism." Evangelicals have a deep "devotion to the Bible," which is a "result of their belief that all spiritual truth is to be found in its pages."[3] Finally, evangelicals emphasize "crucicentrism," that is, they place at "the centre of their theological scheme the doctrine of the cross—the atoning work of Jesus Christ in his death."[4] This "functional definition of evangelicalism" has found widespread scholarly approval and employment.

Puritanism and Evangelicalism: Similarities and Differences

Critical to Bebbington's discussion of evangelicalism is his distinguishing of it from Puritanism, which Bebbington identifies as the "dominant force" within English-speaking Protestantism prior to the emergence of evangelicalism in the eighteenth century.[5] Finding a definition of Puritanism is notoriously difficult. For some students of history, the Puritans are that body of men and women who sought to reform the state church of England between the 1560s, when the term Puritan first appeared in the English language,[6] and 1662, when most of them chose to leave the state church because of what they deemed oppressive legislation. This definition would restrict Puritanism to a reform or renewal movement within sixteenth- and seventeenth-century Anglicanism.

---

[1] David W. Bebbington, "Scottish Cultural Influences on Evangelicalism," *Scottish Bulletin of Evangelical Theology* 14, no. 1 (Spring 1996): 23.

[2] David W. Bebbington, "Evangelical Christianity and the Enlightenment," *Crux* 25, no. 4 (December 1989): 29.

[3] David W. Bebbington, *Evangelicalism in Modern Britain: A History from the 1730s to the 1980s* (1989; repr., Grand Rapids: Baker, 1992), 12.

[4] Bebbington, "Evangelical Christianity and the Enlightenment," 30.

[5] Ibid., 32.

[6] M. M. Knappen, *Tudor Puritanism* (Chicago: University of Chicago Press, 1966), 488.

A more expansive definition, though, sees Puritanism as a movement of spirituality.[7] Whatever else the Puritans may have been—social, political, and ecclesiastical Reformers—they were primarily men and women intensely passionate about piety and Christian experience. In this definition, what united the Puritans was both their doctrine, Calvinism, and their conviction that every aspect of their spiritual lives came from the work of the Holy Spirit. They had, in fact, inherited from the continental Reformers of the sixteenth century, and from John Calvin in particular, "a constant and even distinctive concern" with the person and work of the Holy Spirit.[8]

Benjamin B. Warfield (1851–1921), the distinguished American Presbyterian theologian, has this to say about this Puritan preoccupation: "Puritan thought was almost entirely occupied with loving study of the work of the Holy Spirit, and found its highest expression in dogmatico-practical expositions of the several aspects of it."[9] This view of Puritanism would therefore include within its bounds not only the Puritans who lived and labored within the state church of Anglicanism, but also those who came to populate the major denominational bodies that sought to preserve the theological and spiritual vision of the Anglican Puritans after the Restoration of Charles II in 1660—the English Presbyterians, the Congregationalists, and the Particular (or Calvinistic) Baptists, collectively known as the "Dissenters." According to Bebbington, there is significant continuity between Puritanism and evangelicalism—both are "undoubtedly conversionist, biblicist and crucicentric." But, in his opinion, the former lacked "activism." There were a few exceptions, like John Eliot (1604–1690), who worked

---

[7] Irvonwy Morgan, *Puritan Spirituality* (London: Epworth, 1973), 53–65, esp. 60; Dewey D. Wallace Jr., ed., *The Spirituality of the Later English Puritans: An Anthology* (Macon, GA: Mercer University Press, 1987), xi–xiv; J. I. Packer, *A Quest for Godliness: The Puritan Vision of the Christian Life* (Wheaton, IL: Crossway, 1990), 37–38.

[8] Richard B. Gaffin Jr., "The Holy Spirit," *The Westminster Theological Journal* 43 (1980): 61. See also the detailed discussion by Garth B. Wilson, "Doctrine of the Holy Spirit in the Reformed Tradition: A Critical Overview," in *The Holy Spirit: Renewing and Empowering Presence*, ed. George Vandervelde (Winfield, BC: Wood Lake, 1989), 57–62.

[9] Benjamin B. Warfield, "Introductory Note" to Abraham Kuyper, *The Work of the Holy Spirit* (1900; repr., Grand Rapids: Eerdmans, 1956), xxviii.

among the Native Americans of eastern Massachusetts,[10] but by and large the Puritans and their Dissenting heirs were not engaged in missionary endeavors to areas of the world where the gospel was not known.[11]

Bebbington traces this lack of cross-cultural missions to a particular understanding of the doctrine of assurance. According to Bebbington, the Puritans and Dissenters "held that assurance is rare, late and the fruit of struggle in the experience of believers."[12] Among the proof that he cites for this assertion is the following text from the Westminster Confession of Faith (1646): "Infallible assurance doth not so belong to the essence of faith, but that a true believer may wait long, and conflict with many difficulties before he be partaker of it."[13] The introspective piety fostered by this view of assurance and the energy consumed in seeking to determine whether or not one was among the elect seriously hampered Puritan and Dissenting missionary endeavors. How could the Puritans and Dissenters spread the gospel when they were not even sure that they were saved?

Evangelicals, by contrast, were convinced that "assurance is the normal possession of the believer."[14] The great evangelist of the eighteenth century George Whitefield (1714–1770), reflecting on his conversion in 1735, could state in a letter to fellow evangelist John Wesley (1703–1791) in 1740, "For these five or six years I have received the witness of God's Spirit; since that, blessed be God, I have not doubted a quarter of an hour of a saving interest in Jesus Christ."[15] When Whitefield met the Welsh preacher Howell Harris (1714–1773) for the first time, he reputedly asked the Welshman,

---

[10] For a study of Eliot and his mission, see Richard W. Cogley, "John Eliot's Puritan Ministry," *Fides et Historia* 31, no. 1 (1999): 1–18; and Cogley, *John Eliot's Mission to the Indians before King Philip's War* (Cambridge, MA: Harvard University Press, 1999). For a brief overview of Eliot's ministry, see Hugh Collier, "John Eliot—Apostle to the Indians," *Reformation Trust* 254 (July–August 2013): 17–21.

[11] Bebbington, *Evangelicalism in Modern Britain*, 40–42; Bebbington, "Evangelical Christianity and the Enlightenment," 32.

[12] Bebbington, *Evangelicalism in Modern Britain*, 43.

[13] The Westminster Confession of Faith 18.3.

[14] Bebbington, *Evangelicalism in Modern Britain*, 45.

[15] Quoted in David W. Bebbington, "Revival and Enlightenment in Eighteenth-Century England," in *Modern Christian Revivals*, ed. Edith L. Blumhofer and Randall Balmer (Urbana/Chicago, IL: University of Illinois Press, 1993), 22.

"Do you know your sins are forgiven?"[16] And in an oft-reprinted sermon about the indwelling of the Spirit of God, Whitefield told his hearers that to "say, we may have God's Spirit without feeling it . . . is in reality to deny the thing itself."[17] This robust sense of assurance delivered evangelicals from the introspective piety of the Puritans and enabled them to take up the task of spreading the gospel to others with assiduity and zeal.[18]

Puritan Missions

Were the Puritans, however, so generally devoid of missionary zeal, as Bebbington argues? Bebbington recognizes that there were some Puritans who engaged in itinerant evangelism and that Richard Baxter (1615–1691) longed for the conversion of the nations. But these cases, and that of John Eliot, he holds to be quite unusual.[19] But were they so exceptional? The Puritans, as Bebbington owns, were conversionist. Much of the immense body of sermons that they preached and literature that they wrote was evangelistic in intent.

Consider, for example, John Rogers (c. 1570–1636), whose extraordinary method of preaching earned him the sobriquet "Roaring Rogers," and who had an especially fruitful ministry in the Puritan parish of Dedham, Essex, from 1605 till his death thirty-one years later.[20] Among his few published works was *A Treatise of Love*, which had begun life as a series of sermons on 1 John 3:23 ("This is [God's] commandment, that we believe in the name of his Son Jesus Christ and love one another"), a series preached to a congregation of hundreds who regularly attended his ministry. One of the marks of true love for God, Rogers asserted, is that it

---

[16] Quoted in Arnold A. Dallimore, *George Whitefield: The Life and Times of the Great Evangelist of the Eighteenth-Century Revival*, vol. 1 (1970; repr., Westchester, IL: Cornerstone, 1979), 264.

[17] George Whitefield, "The Indwelling of the Spirit, the Common Privilege of All Believers," in *Sermons on Important Subjects* (London: Thomas Tegg, 1833), 433.

[18] Bebbington, "Revival and Enlightenment in Eighteenth-Century England," 21–22.

[19] Bebbington, *Evangelicalism in Modern Britain*, 34, 40–41.

[20] On Rogers, see Jason Yiannikkou, "Rogers, John (c. 1570–1636)," in *Oxford Dictionary of National Biography* (Oxford: Oxford University Press, 2004), accessed September 15, 2013, http://www.oxforddnb.com .libaccess.lib.mcmaster.ca/view/article/23982; Gerard G. Moate, ed., *The Parish Church of St. Mary [the Virgin], Dedham* (St. Ives, Cornwall, UK: Beric Tempest for Dedham Parish Church Council, n.d.), 6.

longs that others love God as well and so seeks "to draw as many to God" as it can, "as Philip did Nathanael" (see John 1:44–46) and Andrew did Peter (see John 1:40–42).[21] In fact, Christian love has a global reach, for it "reacheth to all, near and far, strangers, enemies, within and without the pale of the Church, Turks [that is, Muslims] and pagans, we must pray for them, & do them any good if they come in our way."[22] In fact, Rogers explicitly urged his readers that "we must pray for the poor pagans, that God would send his light and truth among them, that they in time may be brought into the bosom of the Church, and the sheepfold of Christ Jesus."[23] Before the sending of God's "light and truth" to "the poor pagans," there were the prayers of countless Puritans like Rogers and his hearers, which provided the soil out of which the late eighteenth-century missionary movement emerged.

In the days after the restoration of the monarchy in the person of Charles II, Puritan spirituality placed especially great emphasis on seeking the salvation of the lost.[24] John Janeway (1633–1657) was, in the words of Dewey Wallace, "a paragon of soul winning." Not long after his own conversion he was earnestly seeking the conversion of unsaved family members and fellow students at Cambridge, "desiring to carry as many of them as possibly he could along with him to Heaven."[25] Joseph Alleine (1634–1668), whose *Alarm to Unconverted Sinners* (1672) was a best seller in the eighteenth-century evangelical print culture, considered going to China to preach the gospel.[26] John Bunyan (1628–1688), one of the great Puritan evangelists of the Restoration era, could describe his passion for the salvation of the lost in terms that both Whitefield and Wesley would have gladly owned:

> My great desire in fulfilling my ministry, was, to get into the darkest places in the country, even amongst those people that

---

[21] John Rogers, *A Treatise of Love* (London: N. Newbery, 1629), 18–19.
[22] Ibid., 41.
[23] Ibid., 140.
[24] Dewey D. Wallace, introduction to Wallace, *Spirituality of the Later English Puritans*, xv.
[25] Ibid.
[26] Ibid.

were furthest off of profession; yet not because I could not endure the light (for I feared not to show my Gospel to any) but because I found my spirit leaned most after awakening and converting work, and the Word that I carried did lean itself most that way; yea, so have I strived to preach the Gospel, not where Christ was named, lest I should build upon another man's foundation, Rom. 15.20.

In my preaching I have really been in pain, and have as it were travelled [i.e., travailed] to bring forth children to God; neither could I be satisfied unless some fruits did appear in my work: if I were fruitless it matter'd not who commended me; but if I were fruitful, I cared not who did condemn. I have thought of that, He that winneth souls is wise, Pro. 11.30.

It pleased me nothing to see people drink in opinions if they seemed ignorant of Jesus Christ, and the worth of their own salvation, sound conviction for Sin, especially for unbelief, and an heart set on fire to be saved by Christ, with strong breathings after a truly sanctified soul: that was it that delighted me; those were the souls I counted blessed.[27]

And the New England Puritan Cotton Mather (1663–1728) was convinced that Puritan prayers were vital for the advance of the gospel throughout the world. As he stated in *The Nets of Salvation* (1704):

Praying for souls is a main stroke in the winning of souls. If once the Spirit of grace be poured out upon a soul, that soul is won immediately. . . . Yea, who can tell, how far the prayers of the saints, & of a few saints, may prevail with heaven to obtain that grace, that shall win whole peoples and kingdoms to serve the Lord? . . . It may be, the nations of the world, would quickly be won from the idolatries of paganism, and the impostures of Mahomet, if a Spirit of prayer, were at work among the people of God.[28]

---

[27] *Grace Abounding to the Chief of Sinners*, 289–91, in John Bunyan, *Grace Abounding to the Chief of Sinners*, ed. W. R. Owens (Harmondsworth, UK: Penguin, 1987), 72–73, modernized.

[28] Quoted in Richard F. Lovelace, *The American Pietism of Cotton Mather: Origins of American Evangelicalism* (Grand Rapids: Eerdmans, 1979), 244, modernized.

Granted there were none in the Puritan era with an itinerant ministry comparable to that of George Whitefield,[29] but this does not mean that the Puritans lacked a sense of mission.[30]

Calvinistic Baptist Passion to Win the Lost

An excellent case study for displaying seventeenth-century Puritanism and its missionary passion is the largest group of Baptists of this era, the Particular or Calvinistic Baptists.[31] This group originated within the Puritan movement in London in the 1630s, and by 1644 there were seven Calvinistic churches. That year these churches issued a statement of faith, The First London Confession of Faith, which demonstrated their fundamental solidarity with the Calvinist communities throughout the British Isles and continental Europe. The First London Confession of Faith went through at least two printings that year, and on November 30, 1646, it was reissued in a second edition. This confession became the doctrinal standard for the first period of Calvinistic Baptist advance, which ended in 1660 with the Restoration of Charles II.[32]

During those sixteen years, these Calvinistic Baptists planted over 120 churches throughout England, Wales, and Ireland, a few of which survive to this very day, an example of church growth that should be the envy of evangelicals today.[33] After the restoration of the monarchy in 1660, these Baptists—along with other Puritan groups like the English Presbyterians and Congregation-

---

[29] J. I. Packer, "The Spirit with the Word: The Reformational Revivalism of George Whitefield," in *The Bible, the Reformation and the Church: Essays in Honour of James Atkinson*, ed. W. P. Stephens (Sheffield, UK: Sheffield Academic Press, 1995), 187–89.

[30] John Walsh, "Methodism at the End of the Eighteenth Century," in *A History of the Methodist Church in Great Britain*, ed. Rupert Davies and Gordon Rupp, vol. 1 (London: Epworth, 1965), 293. For a good treatment of the Puritan commitment to mission, see J. I. Packer, "Puritan Evangelism," in *A Quest for Godliness*, 291–308; and Jon Hinkinson, "Missions among Puritans and Pietists," in *The Great Commission: Evangelicals and the History of World Missions*, ed. Martin I. Klauber and Scott M. Manetsch (Nashville, TN: B&H, 2008), 23–34.

[31] For details of the origins of this group, see Michael A. G. Haykin, *Kiffin, Knollys and Keach—Rediscovering Our English Baptist Heritage* (Leeds, UK: Reformation Today, 1996), 26–40.

[32] Murray Tolmie, *The Triumph of the Saints: The Separate Churches of London 1616–1649* (Cambridge: Cambridge University Press, 1977), 61–65; B. R. White, "The Doctrine of the Church in the Particular Baptist Confession of 1644," *The Journal of Theological Studies*, n.s., 19 (1968): 570; White, "The Origins and Convictions of the First Calvinistic Baptists," *Baptist History and Heritage* 25, no. 4 (October 1990): 45.

[33] For the 1660 statistics of churches, see W. T. Whitley, "Baptist Churches till 1660," *Transactions of the Baptist Historical Society* 2 (1910–1911): 236–54.

alists—found themselves heavily persecuted by the state church, which longed to create a culture marked by religious uniformity. Yet, in the midst of this persecution, which lasted till 1688, these Baptists continued to grow and evangelize.

Key to this growth were pastors and evangelists who were passionate about the salvation of the lost. The most significant Baptist theologian of the late seventeenth century was undoubtedly Benjamin Keach (1640–1704).[34] His pulpit ministry was characterized by vigorous evangelism and regular calls to the unconverted to respond to Christ in faith. Here is one example of a number that could be cited:

> Receive this Saviour, believe in him, and you shall be saved whosoever you are. It is not the greatness of your sins that can hinder or obstruct him from saving your souls; though your sins be as red as scarlet, or as red as crimson, he will wash them all away, and shall make you as white as wool, as white as snow.[35]

Keach continued in this vein by means of some comments on Revelation 3:20 ("Behold, I stand at the door and knock. If anyone hears my voice and opens the door, I will come in to him and eat with him, and he with me"):

> Will you not open the door, nor cry to him to help you to open to him, to enable you to believe in him? What do you say, shall the Son of God stand at your doors, and you shall not so much as ask, "Who is there? Who is at my Door?" Shall Christ be kept out of your hearts, and stand at your doors, whilst sin commands the chiefest room, and has absolute power over you,

---

[34] On Keach, see James Barry Vaughn, "Public Worship and Practical Theology in the Work of Benjamin Keach (1640–1704)" (PhD diss., University of St. Andrews, 1989); Austin Walker, *The Excellent Benjamin Keach* (Dundas, ON: Joshua, 2004); James Christopher Holmes, "The Role of Metaphor in the Sermons of Benjamin Keach" (PhD diss., The Southern Baptist Theological Seminary, 2009); Jonathan W. Arnold, "The Reformed Theology of Benjamin Keach" (DPhil diss., Oxford University, 2010); and D. B. Riker, *A Catholic Reformed Theologian: Federalism and Baptism in the Work of Benjamin Keach (1640–1704)*, Studies in Baptist History and Thought 35 (Eugene, OR: Wipf & Stock, 2010).

[35] Benjamin Keach, "The Great Salvation," in *A Golden Mine Opened* (London, 1694), 385. I (Michael Haykin) am indebted for this reference and the one that follows to Rev. Austin Walker of Crawley, England. The capitalization and punctuation in both quotes have been modernized.

and rules in you? How will you be able to look this Blessed Saviour in the face another Day? Is he come through a sea of blood to offer his love to you, and to espouse you unto himself for ever, and will you not be persuaded to break your league with your old lovers, who will at last stab you at the very heart, and betray your souls into the hands of divine wrath? Nay, they have done it already. What are your lovers but your lusts, your pride, your earthly-mindedness, your sinful pleasures, profits and honours? O resolve to desert them, they otherwise will damn your souls for ever, and expose you to the torment of hell-fire . . . to deliver you from them, and from that wrath which is due to you for them, (I mean for your sins) is Christ come, and this great Saviour is offered to you.[36]

According to C. H. Spurgeon (1834–1892)—the famous nineteenth-century Calvinistic Baptist preacher who pastored the congregation that descended from Keach's congregation—in speaking to the lost, Keach was "intensely direct, solemn, and impressive, not flinching to declare the terrors of the Lord, nor veiling the freeness of divine grace."[37] Another typical evangelistic appeal by Keach to the unconverted is the following, cited by Spurgeon to illustrate the above statement:

Come, venture, your souls on Christ's righteousness; Christ is able to save you though you are ever so great sinners. Come to him, throw yourselves at the feet of Jesus. *Look to Jesus*, who came to seek and save them that were lost. . . . You may have the water of life freely. Do not say, "I want qualifications or a meekness to come to Christ." Sinner, dost thou thirst? Dost thou see a want of righteousness? 'Tis not a righteousness; but 'tis a sense of the want of righteousness, which is rather the qualification thou shouldst look at. Christ hath righteousness sufficient to clothe you, bread of life to feed you, grace to adorn you. Whatever you want, it is to be had in him. We tell you there is help in

---

[36] Keach, "The Great Salvation," 386–87.
[37] C. H. Spurgeon, *The Metropolitan Tabernacle: Its History and Work* (London: Passmore and Alabaster, 1876), 31.

him, salvation in him. "Through the propitiation in his blood" you must be justified, and that by faith alone.[38]

But one might say, "All of these examples simply illustrate that Keach had a concern for the salvation of the English and those who sat under the sound of his preaching—what of the rest of the world?" Well, consider one final text, which comes from Keach's poem *War with the Devil*, one of his most popular works during his lifetime. This text is a clear indication that even though Puritans like Keach were unable to go to the places and peoples at "the ends of the earth," his concern for gospel expansion was a global one:

> Let France, dark Spain, and Italy,
> Thy Light and Glory, Lord, behold:
> To each adjacent Countrey
> Do thou the Gospel plain unfold:
> O let thy Face upon them shine,
> That all these Nations may be thine.
>
> Let Christendom new Christ'ned be,
> And unto thee O let them turn,
> And be Baptiz'd, O Christ, by thee
> With th' Spirit of thy Holy One:
> O let thy Face upon it shine,
> That Christendom may all be thine.
>
> And carry on thy glorious Work
> Victoriously in every Land,
> Let Tartars and the mighty Turk
> Subject themselves to thy Command:
> O let thy Face upon them Shine,
> That those blind People may be thine.
>
> And let thy brightness also go,
> To Asia and to Africa,

---

[38] Ibid.

Let Egypt and Assyria too
Submit unto thy blessed Law:
O let thy Face upon them shine,
That those dark Regions may be thine.

Nay, precious God, let Light extend
To China and East-India;
To thee let all the People Bend,
Who live in wild America:
O let thy blessed Gospel shine,
That the blind Heathens may be thine.

Send forth thy Light like to the Morn
Most swiftly, Lord, O let it fly
From Cancer unto Capricorn:
That all dark Nations may espy
Thy glorious Face on them to shine,
And they in Christ for to be thine.[39]

This may not be the best poetry, but the careful delineation of the peoples and places of the world bespeaks a deep concern for the global expansion of the gospel.

If one turns from the fairly well-known figure of Keach to much-lesser-known men among the Calvinistic Baptists, the passion for the advance of the gospel is no different. Consider three sermons, all of them funeral sermons given by the London Baptist John Piggott (d. 1713) in the first decade of the seventeenth century.[40] On the occasion of the death of Thomas Harrison (d. 1702), Piggott closed his funeral sermon with a long and emotional appeal to those

[39] Benjamin Keach, "Divine Breathings," in *War with the Devil*, 8th ed. (London: Benjamin Harris, 1684), 126–27. I (Michael Haykin) owe this reference to one of my doctoral students, Joshua Monroe of Louisville, Kentucky.

[40] John Piggott was a General Baptist who became a Calvinist in the 1690s and founded what became known as Little Wild Street Baptist Church. For an account of his life and ministry, see Joseph Ivimey, *A History of the English Baptists*, vol. 3 (London, 1814), 451–63. For what follows with regard to these three sermons, I (Michael Haykin) am indebted to research carried out by G. Stephen Weaver Jr. of Frankfort, Kentucky, in an unpublished paper, "A Seventeenth Century Baptist View of Ministry as Seen in Three Funeral Sermons by John Piggott" (August 2006), that he submitted to me in a course taught at The Southern Baptist Theological Seminary, "Baptist Theologians in Historical Context."

who had been the regular hearers of his dead friend's preaching, yet who remained unconverted:

> To you that were the constant auditors of the deceas'd minister. Consider how indulgent and favourable God has been to several of you, even in this dark dispensation. He has removed one that was ripe for heaven; but how dismal has been your state, if he had called you that are unprepared! If you drop into the grave while you are unprovided for eternity, you sink beyond the reserves of mercy. O adore the patience and long-suffering of God, that you are yet alive, and have one call more from this pulpit, and another very awful one from the grave of that person who used to fill it. His death calls upon you to repent, and turn to close with Christ, and make sure of heaven. Surely you cannot but feel some emotions in your breasts, when you think you shall never see nor hear your painful[41] minister more. And methinks the rocks within you should flow, when you think that he preached himself to death, and you have not yet entertained that Jesus whom he preached. 'Tis true, God gave him several seals of his ministry, which was the joy of his heart, and will be his crown in the Day of the Lord.
>
> But if you who were only hearers will continue so, he will be a swift witness against you in the Day of God. For tho one place held you and him in this world, you'll have very different habitations in the next. He shall eternally solace himself in boundless rivers of pleasure; but you shall be eternally plunged into a bottomless lake of fire. But let me entreat you by all that is sacred, by the joys of heaven and the torments of hell, by the interest of your never-dying souls, by Christ's bloody sweat in the Garden, and his agony on the cross, that you immediately close with Christ, and receive him as offered in the gospel, submitting to his scepter, as well as depending on his sacrifice, that you may eternally be lodged in the bosom of his love.[42]

---

[41] That is, hard-working.

[42] John Piggott, "A Funeral Sermon Occasion'd by the Death of the Reverend Mr. Thomas Harrison," in *Eleven Sermons Preach'd upon Special Occasions* (London: Cliff and Jackson, 1714), 196–97. The spelling and punctuation of this extract, as well as those that follow, have been modernized.

In his funeral sermon for Hercules Collins (d. 1702),[43] who died on October 4, less than two months after Harrison, Piggott also commented upon the evangelistic zeal of Collins by saying that "no Man could preach with a more affectionate regard to the salvation of souls."[44] Later in this sermon Piggott called on the regular hearers in Collins's church who remained unsaved to be witnesses to the gospel fervor of the deceased preacher: "You are witnesses with what zeal and fervour, with what constancy and seriousness he used to warn and persuade you."[45] At this point Piggott himself could not hold back from crying out, "Tho you have been deaf to his former preaching, yet listen to the voice of this providence, lest you continue in your slumber till you sleep the sleep of death." And he closed with these forceful words:

> You cannot but see, unless you will close your eyes, that this world and the fashion of it is passing away. O what a change will a few months or years make in this numerous assembly! Yea, what a sad change has little more than a fortnight made in this congregation! He that was so lately preaching in this pulpit, is now wrapped in his shroud, and confined to his coffin; and the lips that so often dispersed knowledge amongst you, are sealed up till the resurrection.
>
> Here's the body of your late minister; but his soul is entered into the joy of his Lord. O that those of you that would not be persuaded by him living, might be wrought upon by his death![46]

As in his funeral sermon for Thomas Harrison, Piggott's own passion for the salvation of souls is clearly visible in the way in which he addressed the unconverted.

---

[43] On Collins, see Michael A. G. Haykin and Steve Weaver, *"Devoted to the Service of the Temple": Piety, Persecution, and Ministry in the Writings of Hercules Collins* (Grand Rapids: Reformation Heritage, 2007); and G. Stephen Weaver Jr., "Hercules Collins: Orthodox, Puritan, Baptist" (PhD diss., The Southern Baptist Theological Seminary, 2013).

[44] John Piggott, "A Sermon Preach'd at the Funeral of the Reverend Mr. Hercules Collins," in *Eleven Sermons*, 236.

[45] Ibid., 240.

[46] Ibid.

Finally, in his funeral sermon for William Collins (d. 1702), which Piggott was called upon to preach but three weeks after the one he gave for Hercules Collins, Piggott asserted that the main burden of William Collins's preaching had to do with a free gospel proclamation rooted in his love for sinners:

> The subjects he ordinarily insisted on in the course of his ministry, were the great and important truths of the Gospel, which he handled with great judgment and clearness. How would he open the miseries of the fall! And in how moving a manner would he discourse of the excellency of Christ, and the virtues of his blood, and his willingness to save poor awakened burdened sinners![47]

When Piggott himself died in 1713, his funeral sermon was preached by Joseph Stennett I (1663–1713), a leading London Calvinistic Baptist divine.[48] Stennett is usually remembered today for a number of his hymns that the so-called father of English hymnody, Isaac Watts (1674–1748), found inspirational. Among his lesser-known hymns is a baptismal hymn in which Stennett makes explicit reference to Matthew 28:19–20, the Great Commission, in three of the stanzas. Immediately before these stanzas, though, he sums up Christ's missionary command to his apostles as an "Order to convert the World."[49] Again, it would be easy to regard the texts cited above about Stennett's contemporaries as simply revealing a concern for local evangelism. But this line from Stennett gives voice to a consciousness to take the gospel beyond their British horizon.

Matthew 28:19–20 was usually cited by seventeenth-century

---

[47] John Piggott, "A Sermon Preach'd at the Funeral of the Reverend Mr. William Collins," in *Eleven Sermons*, 280–81.

[48] For the life and ministry of Stennett, see especially "Some Account of the Life of the Reverend and Learned Mr. Joseph Stennett," in *The Works of the Late Reverend and Learned Mr. Joseph Stennett*, vol. 1 (London, 1732), 3–36; Allen Harrington and Martha Stennett Harrington, "The Stennetts of England," accessed August 30, 2013, http://www.blue-hare.com/stennett/tpgindex.htm#prefixa; S. L. Copson, "Stennett, Joseph (1663–1713)," in *Oxford Dictionary of National Biography* (Oxford University Press, 2004); online ed., May 2006, accessed August 11, 2012, http://www.oxforddnb.com.libaccess.lib.mcmaster.ca/view/article/26360; Michael A. G. Haykin, "'At Thy Table . . . Thy Loveliness I View': The Person of Jesus Christ in the Hymns of Joseph Stennett I," *The Baptist Quarterly* 45, no. 2 (April 2013): 69–86.

[49] Joseph Stennett, "The Sacred Body of Our Lord," in *Hymns Compos'd for the Celebration of the Holy Ordinance of Baptism* (London: Darby, 1712), 4 (hymn 2, stanza 3).

Baptists in their defense of believer's baptism. For instance, William Kiffin (1616–1701), Hanserd Knollys (1599–1691), and Benjamin Coxe (fl. 1640–1660) stated:

> The only written commission to baptize (which is in Matth. 28:19.) directeth us to baptize disciples only, *Go ye and disciple all nations, baptizing them*; that is, the disciples: for this is the only construction and interpretation that the Greek word can there bear; and infants cannot be made disciples, because they cannot learn.
>
> . . . Then only is baptism administered according to the rule of the Word, when a disciple is baptized into the name of the Father, and of the Son, etc. Matth. 28:19, that is, into the profession of faith in the Father, Son, and holy Spirit; . . . this necessarily excludes infants, who can make no such profession.[50]

Only those who are disciples, that is, those who have heard the gospel, learned of Christ, and responded to it in faith and repentance, should be baptized.

As noted, this is the most common way that seventeenth-century Calvinistic Baptists employed this passage. However, a sermon on this text from Matthew 28 was preached in 1700 by a certain John Williams after a public debate in Portsmouth between him, along with some other Baptists, and some Paedobaptists. Williams emphasized that the command to teach and baptize disciples concerned "all nations" and that the command was not restricted to the apostles who saw the risen Christ.[51] The only restriction that Williams allowed was the working of providence: the gospel is to go "to all nations, as providence should direct them [that is, the preachers], and open a door to them."[52]

---

[50] William Kiffin, Hanserd Knollys, and Benjamin Coxe, *A Declaration Concerning the Publike Dispute* . . . *Concerning Infants-Baptisme* (London, 1645), 19–20. Spelling and punctuation have been modernized.
[51] John Williams, *A Sermon Preach'd from the Commission, Matth. 28.19* (London, 1700), 136–38.
[52] Ibid., 138.

5

"Advancing the Kingdom of Christ"

MISSIONAL PRAYING—THE EXAMPLE
OF JONATHAN EDWARDS

Few remember Jonathan Edwards today as being missions minded, and in the minds of many, surely his deep commitment to a Calvinist worldview effectively hindered the formulation of a rich missionary vision. In an article published in the late 1970s, for instance, James Manor stated, "Edwards himself was too close to traditional calvinism [sic] and too concerned with the defense of the sovereignty of God against the arminians [sic] to be termed a mission activist." Manor did admit that Edwards's writings were a catalyst for the thinking of Calvinist missionaries like William Carey.[1] But how mistaken is his thinking about Edwards himself!

First, Edwards actually served as a missionary. During his time in Stockbridge in the heart of the Berkshire Mountains of Massachusetts, Edwards was a missionary to some 250 Mohican and 60

---

[1] James Manor, "The Coming of Britain's Age of Empire and Protestant Mission Theology, 1750–1839," *Zeitschrift für Missionswissenschaft und Religionswissenschaft* 61 (1977): 43. Manor devotes five pages to the examination of Edwards's thought in this regard (39–43).

Mohawk Indians.[2] Clear evidence from a literary perspective that his missionary life in Stockbridge has not been appreciated is the fact that up until 1999, not one of the sermons that he preached to the Stockbridge Indians had been published.[3] Yet, as George Marsden, Edwards's most recent biographer, has noted, Edwards's preeminent goal during his time at Stockbridge was to reach these Indians with the life-giving gospel.[4]

Then, too, when examination of Edwards's theological vision is made, it is seen to be a global vision, in which, as he looked to the future, he saw ever-increasing victories in the missionary advance of the kingdom of Christ.[5] Let us look at Edwards's missionary thought in more detail.

The *Personal Narrative*

Edwards's vision of the missionary growth of the kingdom of Christ had been with him since his earliest pastorate in New York from 1722 to 1723. For example, in the *Personal Narrative*, a text that he drew up probably in 1740 but which reflects experiences at least twenty years prior, Edwards notes of his early days as a believer:

> I had great longings for the advancement of Christ's kingdom in the world. My secret prayer used to be in great part taken up in praying for it. If I heard the least hint of anything that happened in any part of the world, that appeared to me, in some respect or other, to have a favourable aspect on the interest of

---

[2] See Stephen J. Nichols, "Last of the Mohican Missionaries: Jonathan Edwards at Stockbridge," in *The Legacy of Jonathan Edwards: American Religion and the Evangelical Tradition*, ed. D. G. Hart, Sean Michael Lucas, and Stephen J. Nichols (Grand Rapids: Baker, 2003), 47–63.

[3] For two of the sermons to the Stockbridge Indians that have been published, see "To the Mohawks at the Treath, August 16, 1751," and "He That Believeth Shall Be Saved," in *The Sermons of Jonathan Edwards: A Reader*, ed. Wilson H. Kimnach, Kenneth P. Minkema, and Douglas A. Sweeney (New Haven, CT: Yale University Press, 1999), 105–20.

[4] George Marsden, *Jonathan Edwards: A Life* (New Haven, CT: Yale University Press, 2003), 408–9.

[5] See Ronald E. Davies, "Prepare Ye the Way of the Lord: The Missiological Thought and Practice of Jonathan Edwards (1703–1758)" (PhD diss., Fuller Theological Seminary, 1989); Davies, "Jonathan Edwards: Missionary Biographer, Theologian, Strategist, Administrator, Advocate—and Missionary," *International Bulletin of Missionary Research* 21, no. 2 (April 1997): 60–67; Davies, "Jonathan Edwards, Theologian of the Missionary Awakening," EMA Occasional Paper 3, *Evangel* 17, no. 1 (Spring 1999); Davies, *A Heart for Mission: Five Pioneer Thinkers* (Fearn, Tain, Ross-shire: Christian Focus, 2002), 79–96. See also the very important study by Jonathan Gibson, "Jonathan Edwards: A *Missionary*?," *Themelios* 36 (2011): 380–402.

Christ's kingdom, my soul eagerly catched at it; and it would much animate and refresh me.

. . . I very frequently used to retire into a solitary place, on the banks of Hudson's River, at some distance from the city, for contemplation on divine things, and secret converse with God; and had many sweet hours there. Sometimes Mr. Smith and I walked there together, to converse of the things of God; and our conversation used much to turn on the advancement of Christ's kingdom in the world, and the glorious things that God would accomplish for his church in the latter days.[6]

As this text details, private prayer and "sweet hours" of personal conversation were vehicles for Edwards's missionary longings. Reading and Scripture meditation were also focused in this direction, as another extract from the *Personal Narrative* reveals:

My heart has been much on the advancement of Christ's kingdom in the world. The histories of the past advancement of Christ's kingdom, have been sweet to me. When I have read histories of past ages, the pleasantest thing in all my reading has been, to read of the kingdom of Christ being promoted. . . . And my mind has been much entertained and delighted, with the Scripture promises and prophecies, of the future glorious advancement of Christ's kingdom on earth.[7]

What is also noteworthy about both of these texts is the Christ-centeredness of Edwards's global vision. It was the "advancement of Christ's kingdom" for which he ardently longed.[8]

Letters to George Whitefield

Another text, written around the time of the *Personal Narrative*, gives us further insight into Edwards's passion for missions. On February 12, 1740, Edwards wrote a letter to George Whitefield, the

---

[6] Jonathan Edwards, *Personal Narrative*, in *Jonathan Edwards: Letters and Personal Writings*, ed. George S. Claghorn, vol. 16 of *The Works of Jonathan Edwards* (New Haven, CT: Yale University Press, 1998), 797. For the date of the *Personal Narrative*, see *Jonathan Edwards: Letters and Personal Writings*, 747.
[7] Ibid., 800.
[8] Davies, *Heart for Mission*, 82.

English evangelist who was signally used by God in the transat-
lantic revivals of the eighteenth century. Edwards scholar George S.
Claghorn offers a succinct description of Whitefield's impact under
God that is well worth quoting: "Wherever he went [from Georgia
to Maine], he drew congregations by the hundreds and thousands.
Wholesale conversions followed, lives were transformed, and a last-
ing impact was made on the character of the American people."[9]
Edwards's 1740 letter to Whitefield communicated his hope that
Whitefield would be able to visit Northampton on his second trip to
America, a hope that was fulfilled later in the year when the English-
man visited Northampton from Friday, October 17, until Monday,
October 20, and spoke six times, in both public and private settings,
to Edwards's Northampton church. Edwards mentioned in the letter
of invitation that his own soul had been deeply refreshed to hear of

> one raised up in the Church of England to revive the mysteri-
> ous, spiritual, despised, and exploded doctrines of the gospel,
> and full of a spirit of zeal for the promotion of real vital piety,
> whose labours have been attended with such success. Blessed
> be God that hath done it! who is with you, and helps you and
> makes the weapons of your warfare mighty.[10]

Edwards expressed a hope that this was the "dawning of a day of
God's almighty power and glorious grace to the world of mankind."
The New England theologian then prayed that God would

> send forth more labourers into his harvest of a like spirit [to
> Whitefield], until the kingdom of Satan shall shake, and his
> proud empire fall throughout the earth and the kingdom of
> Christ, that glorious kingdom of light, holiness, peace and love,
> shall be established from one end of the earth unto the other![11]

In Edwards's mind, central to the advance of the kingdom of Christ
were powerful preachers like Whitefield, whose Spirit-anointed

---

[9] *Jonathan Edwards: Letters and Personal Writings*, 79.
[10] Ibid., 80.
[11] Ibid., 81.

preaching would be used by God to bring down the empire of Satan around the globe.

This need for such Spirit-anointed preaching in pushing forward the boundaries of Christ's kingdom comes to the fore in a second letter to Whitefield that year. Edwards asked the English evangelist to pray for him so that Edwards might be, as he put it, "filled with his [that is, God's] Spirit, and may become fervent, as a flame of fire in my work, and may be abundantly succeeded, and that it would please God, however unworthy I am, to improve me as an instrument of his glory, and advancing the kingdom of Christ."[12]

All of the texts by Edwards so far cited also breathe a strong optimism that some Christians today may not wish to adopt, namely, Edwards's postmillennialism, which is never far from the surface when he is thinking about missions.[13] However, as Ron Davies comments, whatever our eschatological orientation, "we may have a similar confidence in the power of God and expect greater success in the preaching of the Gospel . . . than we often do."[14] And we can wholeheartedly embrace Edwards's conviction that the missionary advance of Christ's kingdom is intimately linked to prayer and preaching.

The Example of David Brainerd

Another very significant text needs to be considered briefly with regard to Edwards's missionary thought, and that is his biography of David Brainerd (1718–1747). Brainerd was a young missionary to native North American Indians in New York, Pennsylvania, and New Jersey, who died of tuberculosis in Edwards's own home. Edwards inherited all of Brainerd's literary remains, and soon after Brainerd's death he began shaping them into the biographical narrative that successive generations have known as *An Account of the Life of the Late Reverend Mr. David Brainerd*. This work first ap-

---

[12] Jonathan Edwards, letter to George Whitefield, December 14, 1740, in ibid., 87.
[13] On his eschatology, see Davies, "Jonathan Edwards: Missionary Biographer," 64–65; Davies, *Heart for Mission*, 87–95; Mark C. Rogers, "A Missional Eschatology: Jonathan Edwards, Future Prophecy, and the Spread of the Gospel," *Fides et Historia* 41, no. 1 (Winter/Spring 2009): 23–46.
[14] Davies, *Heart for Mission*, 88–89.

peared in 1749 and has never been out of print. It is undoubtedly one of Edwards's most important books.[15]

In it Edwards sought to accomplish two ends: display a model of authentic spirituality—for a concern had arisen during the Great Awakening about the nature of true piety—and recommend "a self-denying missionary sensibility" or mind-set.[16] In the latter aim, Edwards succeeded far better than he knew. As Joseph Conforti has observed, the book "had its greatest impact on [nineteenth-century] American missionaries."[17] For Edwards, Brainerd was a constant reminder of the sort of missionary that the church needs. He was a man, in Edwards's words, "who had indeed sold all for Christ and had entirely devoted himself to God, and made his glory his highest end."[18]

The *Humble Attempt*

As Edwards reflected on the endeavor of missions, he came increasingly to believe that corporate prayer was vital for the missionary expansion of the kingdom of Christ.[19] While in some respects he was an innovator in his own time with regard to corporate prayer meetings, what he called "concerts of prayer," there was some Puritan precedent. For example, the New England Puritan Cotton Mather believed that the vitality of the church in any era is, in the final analysis, dependent on the Holy Spirit's sovereign power. He thus maintained that the most significant practical response to the spiritual decline of his day was concerted prayer for the Spirit to save sinners, not only in New England, but throughout the world.[20] In 1706, Mather published a booklet, *Private Meetings Animated and*

---

[15] For studies of this work, see Joseph Conforti, "Jonathan Edwards's Most Popular Work: The Life of David Brainerd and Nineteenth Century Evangelical Culture," *Church History* 54 (1985): 188–201; David B. Calhoun, "David Brainerd: 'A Constant Stream,'" *Presbyterion* 13 (1987): 44–50; Gary Brady, "Books in History: Edwards on David Brainerd," *The Evangelical Library Bulletin* 97 (Winter 1996): 6–8.

[16] Conforti, "Jonathan Edwards's Most Popular Work," 197. See also Davies, *Heart for Mission*, 85.

[17] Conforti, "Jonathan Edward's Most Popular Work," 196.

[18] Jonathan Edwards, "A Sermon Preached on the Day of the Funeral of the Rev. Mr. David Brainerd," in *The Life of David Brainerd*, ed. Norman Pettit, vol. 7 of *The Works of Jonathan Edwards* (New Haven, CT: Yale University Press, 1985), 548.

[19] Rogers, "A Missional Eschatology," 42–45.

[20] See chap. 4, at note 28.

Regulated, in which he encouraged believers to meet in small groups so that, among other things, "their fervent supplications" would hopefully result in "the Spirit of Grace [being] mightily poured out upon the rising generation." Mather recommended bimonthly meetings in which the whole evening could be devoted "unto supplications for the conversion and salvation of the rising generation in the land; and particularly for the success of the Gospel in that congregation" to which the members of the prayer meeting belonged.[21]

Edwards's involvement in the Northampton revival of 1734–1735 and the Great Awakening of 1740–1742 left him with the keen conviction that the advance of God's kingdom in history was intimately connected to times of revival. The New England divine was also certain that prayer for these times of revival was central to seeing them take place. Thus he drew up and published in 1748 a treatise that sought to encourage believers to gather together regularly to pray for the pouring out of God's Spirit. Entitled *An Humble Attempt to Promote Explicit Agreement and Visible Union of God's People in Extraordinary Prayer, for the Revival of Religion and the Advancement of Christ's Kingdom on Earth, pursuant to Scripture-Promises and Prophecies concerning the Last Time* (henceforth referred to simply as the *Humble Attempt*), the treatise is well summed up by a sentence near the beginning of the work:

> It is a very suitable thing, and well-pleasing to God, for many people, in different parts of the world, by express agreement, to come into a visible union in extraordinary, speedy, fervent, and constant prayer, for those great effusions of the Holy Spirit, which shall bring on that advancement of Christ's church and kingdom, that God has so often promised shall be in the latter ages of the world.[22]

This treatise would have some impact during Edwards's own lifetime, but its main influence came during the final decades of

---

[21] Cotton Mather, *Private Meetings Animated and Regulated* (Boston, 1706), 10–11, 19.

[22] Jonathan Edwards, *Humble Attempt*, in *Apocalyptic Writings*, ed. Stephen J. Stein, vol. 5 of *The Works of Jonathan Edwards* (New Haven: Yale University Press, 1977), 320.

the eighteenth century, when it was instrumental in kindling a profoundly significant revival among the Calvinistic Baptists of Great
Britain and in initiating the modern missionary movement, as well
as the Second Great Awakening.[23]

The *Humble Attempt* itself was inspired by information that Edwards received during the course of 1745 about a prayer movement
for revival that had been formed by a number of Scottish evangelical ministers. These ministers and their congregations had agreed to
spend a part of Saturday evening and Sunday morning each week,
as well as the first Tuesday of February, May, August, and November, in prayer to God for "an abundant effusion of his Holy Spirit"
so as to "revive true religion in all parts of Christendom, and to
deliver all nations from their great and manifold spiritual calamities
and miseries, and bless them with the unspeakable benefits of the
kingdom of our glorious Redeemer, and fill the whole earth with
his glory."[24] This "concert of prayer" ran for an initial two years
and then was renewed for a further seven.

When Edwards was sent information regarding this Scottish concert of prayer, he lost no time in seeking to implement a similar concert of prayer in the New England colonies. He encouraged his own
congregation to get involved and also communicated the concept of
such a prayer union to neighboring ministers who he felt would be
receptive to the idea. Although the idea initially met with a poor response, Edwards refused to be put off. In a sermon that he preached
in February 1747 on Zechariah 8:20–22, he sought to demonstrate
how the Old Testament text supported his call for a union of praying
Christians. Within the year a revised and greatly expanded version
of this sermon was ready for publication as the *Humble Attempt*.

The book is divided into three parts. The first section opens
with a number of observations on Zechariah 8:20–22 and then goes
on to provide a description of the origin of the concert of prayer in
Scotland. From the text in Zechariah, Edwards inferred that

---

[23] See Michael A. G. Haykin, *One Heart and One Soul: John Sutcliff of Olney, His Friends and His Times* (Darlington, UK: Evangelical Press, 1994), 153–71.
[24] Edwards, *Humble Attempt*, 321.

there shall be given much of a spirit of prayer to God's people, in many places, disposing them to come into an express agreement, unitedly to pray to God in an extraordinary manner, that he would appear for the help of his church, and in mercy to mankind, and pour out his Spirit, revive his work, and advance his spiritual kingdom in the world, as he has promised.[25]

Edwards thus concluded that it is a duty well pleasing to God and incumbent upon God's people in America to assemble and, with "extraordinary, speedy, fervent and constant prayer," pray for those "great effusions of the Holy Spirit" that will dramatically advance the kingdom of Christ.

Part 2 of the treatise cites a number of reasons for participating in the concert of prayer. Our Lord Jesus shed his blood and tears, and poured out his prayers to secure the blessed presence of his Spirit for all of his elect and the establishment of his kingdom around the world. "The sum of the blessings Christ sought," wrote Edwards, "by what he did and suffered in the work of redemption, was the Holy Spirit." He continued,

The Holy Spirit, in his indwelling, his influences and fruits, is the sum of all grace, holiness, comfort and joy, or in one word, of all the spiritual good Christ purchased for men in this world: and is also the sum of all perfection, glory and eternal joy, that he purchased for them in another world.[26]

Therefore, Edwards rightly concluded, if this is what Christ longed for and "set his heart upon, from all eternity, and which he did and suffered so much for, offering up 'strong crying and tears' [Heb. 5:7], and his precious blood to obtain it; surely his disciples and members should also earnestly seek it, and be much and earnest in prayer for it."[27]

Edwards pointed out, moreover, that Scripture is replete with commands, incentives, and illustrations regarding prayer for the

---

[25] Ibid., 317.
[26] Ibid., 341.
[27] Ibid., 344.

Holy Spirit. There is, for example, the encouragement given in Luke 11:13.[28] These words of Christ, Edwards observed, imply that prayer for the Holy Spirit is one request that God the Father is particularly pleased to answer in the affirmative. Or one might consider the example of the early disciples, who devoted themselves to "united fervent prayer and supplication . . . till the Spirit came down in a wonderful manner upon them," as it is related in Acts 1–2.[29]

Part 3 is the longest portion of the *Humble Attempt* and is devoted to answering various objections to the idea of a concert of prayer. Edwards devoted the bulk of this section to proving his case from a postmillennial reading of the New Testament eschatology. But he also had to answer the accusation that the concert of prayer was something previously unknown in the history of the church and was thus suspect. In actual fact, as we have seen with Cotton Mather, there had been advocates for such meetings from the early years of the eighteenth century. Edwards made no mention of Mather, but he did recall that in 1712 a group of London Dissenters had issued *A Serious Call from the City to the Country*, in which it was urged that an extra hour be set aside every week to beseech God to "appear for the Deliverance and Enlargement of His Church."[30]

The Legacy of the *Humble Attempt*

A significant number of congregations in America and Scotland observed concerts of prayer throughout the 1750s. Especially during the French and Indian War (1755–1760), when the British and the French were fighting for the hegemony of North America, the concert of prayer was in wide use among American Calvinists. In 1759, for instance, Robert Smith informed fellow Presbyterians in Pennsylvania that the concert of prayer would prove to be far

---

[28] "If ye then, being evil, know how to give good gifts unto your children: how much more shall your heavenly Father give the Holy Spirit to them that ask him?" (KJV).

[29] Edwards, *Humble Attempt*, 347–48, 356.

[30] Ibid., 428; Michael J. Crawford, *Seasons of Grace: Colonial New England's Revival Tradition in Its British Context* (New York: Oxford University Press, 1991), 41–42, 229.

more effective in hastening the "brightest period of the militant Church's glory" than the military victories won by British forces.[31] Yet, as has been noted, the *Humble Attempt* would bear its greatest fruit some twenty-five years after the death of its author, and that among the Calvinistic Baptists of Great Britain, whose seventeenth-century forebears we looked at in the previous chapter. Calvinistic Baptists like William Carey and Samuel Pearce (whose missionary passion we document in the next chapter) were deeply shaped by Edwards's thinking about prayer as the engine behind missions, and in this way Edwards became the main theological figure behind many of the great missionary movements of the nineteenth century.

---

[31] Alan Heimert, *Religion and the American Mind: From the Great Awakening to the Revolution* (Cambridge, MA: Harvard University Press, 1966), 366.

6

"An Instrument of Establishing the Empire of My Dear Lord"

DEVELOPING A MISSIONAL PASSION— THE WAY OF SAMUEL PEARCE

Though scarcely known today, Samuel Pearce was in his own day well known for the anointing that attended his preaching and for the depth of his spirituality.[1] It was said of him that "his ardour . . . gave him a kind of ubiquity; as a man and a preacher, he was known, he was felt everywhere."[2] William Jay (1769–1853), who exercised an influential ministry in Bath for the first half of the nineteenth century, said of his contemporary's preaching, "When I have endeavoured to form an image of our Lord as a preacher, Pearce has oftener presented himself to my mind than any other I have been acquainted with." He had, Jay went on, a "mildness and

---

[1] For a study of Pearce, see Michael A. G. Haykin, *Joy Unspeakable and Full of Glory: The Piety of Samuel and Sarah Pearce* (Kitchener, ON: Joshua, 2012).
[2] F. A. Cox, *History of the Baptist Missionary Society, from 1792 to 1842*, vol. 1 (London: T. Ward/G. J. Dyer, 1842), 54.

tenderness" in his style of preaching, and a "peculiar unction." Jay wrote these words many years after Pearce's death, but still, he said, he could picture Pearce in his mind's eye and feel the impression that he made upon his hearers as he preached. Ever one to appreciate the importance of having spiritual individuals as one's friends, Jay made this comment about the last time that he saw Pearce alive: "What a savour does communion with such a man leave upon the spirit."[3]

David Bogue and James Bennett, in their history of the Dissenting interest in England up to the early nineteenth century, have similar remarks about Pearce. When he preached, they said, "the most careless were attentive, the most prejudiced became favourable, and the coldest felt that, in spite of themselves, they began to kindle." But it was when he prayed in public, they remarked, that Pearce's spiritual ardor was most apparent. Then the "most devout were so elevated beyond their former heights, that they said, 'We scarcely ever seemed to pray before.'"[4] In fact, for some decades after his death it was not uncommon to hear him referred to as the "seraphic Pearce."[5]

"Life in a Dear Dying Redeemer"

Pearce was born in Plymouth on July 20, 1766, to devout Baptist parents.[6] His mother died when he was but an infant, and so he was raised by his godly father, William Pearce (d. 1805) and an equally pious grandfather. Young Samuel would also have known the nurturing influence of the "sturdy Baptist community" of Plymouth, whose history reached back well into the seventeenth century.[7]

---

[3] *The Autobiography of William Jay*, ed. George Redford and John Angell James (1854; repr., Edinburgh: Banner of Truth, 1974), 372, 373.
[4] David Bogue and James Bennett, *The History of Dissenters*, 2nd ed., vol. 2 (London: Frederick Westley and A. H. Davis, 1833), 653.
[5] See, for example, *The Life and Letters of John Angell James*, ed. R. W. Dale, 3rd ed. (London: James Nisbet, 1861), 67; John Angell James, *An Earnest Ministry the Want of the Times*, 4th ed. (London: Hamilton, Adams, 1848), 272. The phrase appears to have originated with Pearce's friend John Ryland Jr.: see Ernest A. Payne, "Samuel Pearce," in *The First Generation: Early Leaders of the Baptist Missionary Society in England and America* (London: Carey, 1936), 46.
[6] "Memoir of the Late Rev. Samuel Pearce, A.M.," *The Evangelical Magazine* 8 (1800): 177.
[7] Payne, "Samuel Pearce," 47.

As Pearce came into his teen years, however, he consciously spurned the rich heritage of his godly home and the Plymouth Baptist community. According to his own testimony, "several vicious school-fellows" became his closest friends, and he set his heart on what he would later describe as "evil" and "wicked inclinations."[8] But God had better plans for his life. In the summer of 1782, a young preacher by the name of Isaiah Birt (1758–1837) came to preach for a few Sundays in the Plymouth meetinghouse.[9] The Spirit of God drove home Birt's words to Pearce's heart. The change in Pearce from what he later called "a state of death in trespasses and sins" to a "life in a dear dying Redeemer" was sudden but genuine and lasting.[10] After his conversion Pearce was especially conscious of the Spirit's witness within his heart that he was a child of God, and of being "filled with peace and joy unspeakable."[11] A year or so later, on the day when he celebrated his seventeenth birthday, he was baptized as a believer and joined the Plymouth congregation in which he had been raised.

Not long after his baptism the church perceived that Pearce had been endowed with definite gifts that marked him out as one called to pastoral ministry. His church recommended that he pursue a course of study at the Bristol Baptist Academy. From August 1786 to May 1789 Pearce thus studied at what was then the sole Baptist institution in Great Britain for the training of ministers for the Calvinistic Baptist denomination. The benefits afforded by this period of study left him ever grateful. There was, for example, the privilege of studying under Caleb Evans (1737–1791), principal of the academy, and Robert Hall Jr. (1764–1831)—the former a key figure in the late eighteenth-century Calvinistic Baptist community, and the latter a reputed genius who was destined to become one of the great preachers of the early decades of the next century.

---

[8] Andrew Fuller, *Memoirs of the Late Rev. Samuel Pearce, A.M.*, 2nd ed. (Clipstone: J. W. Morris, 1801), 1–2; henceforth cited as *Memoirs of the Late Rev. Samuel Pearce* (2nd ed.).

[9] For the life of Birt, see the memoir by his son: John Birt, "Memoir of the Late Rev. Isaiah Birt," *The Baptist Magazine* 30 (1838): 54–59, 107–16, 197–203.

[10] Samuel Pearce, letter to Isaiah Birt, October 27, 1782, *The Evangelical Magazine* 15 (1807): 111.

[11] Fuller, *Memoirs of the Late Rev. Samuel Pearce* (2nd ed.), 2–3.

Then there were the opportunities for the students to preach and try their wings, as it were. A number of years later Pearce recalled one occasion when he went to evangelize some colliers of Coleford, Gloucestershire, the town in which his father in the faith, Isaiah Birt, had grown up. Standing on a three-legged stool in a hut, he directed thirty or forty of these miners to "the Lamb of God which taketh away the sin of the world." "Such an unction from above" attended his preaching that day that the entirety of his hearers were "melted into tears" and he too, "weeping among them, could scarcely speak . . . for interrupting sighs and sobs."

"For God's Glory, for the Good of Precious Souls"

Early in 1789 Pearce received and accepted a call to serve for a year's probation as the pastor of Cannon Street Baptist Church in Birmingham. He had supplied the Birmingham pulpit the previous summer, as well as over the Christmas vacation. Impressed by Pearce's evangelistic zeal—a number were saved on both occasions—along with his ability to edify God's people, the church sent their request to him in early February 1789. Five weeks later Pearce wrote back consenting to their request, and by June, his studies finished, he was with them.[12] The following year he was formally called to be the pastor of what would turn out to be his only pastoral charge. In his letter of acceptance, written on July 18, 1790, he told the Birmingham Baptists that he hoped the union between pastor and church would "be for God's glory, for the good of precious souls, for your prosperity as a Church, and for my prosperity as your minister."[13] It is noteworthy that he placed "God's glory" in first place. If there was any concern that set the fundamental tone for his ministry, it was this desire to see God glorified in his life and labors. It is also noteworthy that he asked to be given a yearly holiday of six weeks so that he could visit his father in Plymouth.[14]

---

[12] S. Pearce Carey, *Samuel Pearce, M.A., The Baptist Brainerd*, 3rd ed. (London: Carey, n.d.), 93–94.
[13] Ibid., 95.
[14] Ibid., 48–49.

Pearce's ministry at Cannon Street occupied ten all-too-brief years. Yet they were ones of great fruitfulness. No fewer than 335 individuals were converted under his ministry, baptized, and received into the membership of Cannon Street. This figure does not include those converted under his preaching who, for one reason or another, did not join themselves to the Birmingham cause. A Sunday school was started in 1795 and within a very short period of time grew to the point that some twelve hundred scholars were enrolled in it.[15]

At the heart of Pearce's preaching and spirituality was a keynote of eighteenth-century evangelicalism, the mercy of God displayed in the cross of Christ. Writing one Sunday afternoon to William Summers, a friend then residing in London, Pearce told him that he had for his sermon that evening "the best subject of all in the Bible. Eph. i.7—Redemption! how welcome to the captive! Forgiveness! how delightful to the guilty! Grace! how pleasant to the heart of a saved sinner!" Christ's atoning death for sinners, he went on to say, is "the leading truth in the N.T., . . . a doctrine I cannot but venerate; and to the Author of such a redemption my whole soul labours to exhaust itself in praise."[16] And in his final letter to his congregation, written on May 31, 1799, he reminded them that the gospel which he had preached among them for ten years and in which he urged them to stand fast was "the gospel of the grace of God; the gospel of free, full, everlasting salvation, founded on the sufferings and death of God, *manifest in the flesh.*"[17]

Only a handful of Pearce's sermons were published, along with the circular letter for the Midland Baptist Association that he drew up in 1795, entitled *The Doctrine of Salvation by Free Grace Alone.* The latter provides an excellent vantage point from which to view Pearce's Calvinism. Consider the following extract:

---

[15] Ibid., 113; Arthur S. Langley, *Birmingham Baptists: Past and Present* (London: Kingsgate, 1939), 34. Even after Pearce's death, his wife Sarah could rejoice in people joining the church who had been saved under her husband's ministry. See Andrew Fuller, "To the Church in Cannon-Street," in *Memoirs of the Late Rev. Samuel Pearce, A.M.*, rev. ed. (Philadelphia: American Sunday School Union, 1829), 111.

[16] Carey, *Samuel Pearce*, 97–98.

[17] Fuller, *Memoirs of the Late Rev. Samuel Pearce* (2nd ed.), 123–24; see also 140–41.

The point of difference between us and many other profess-
ing Christians lies in the doctrine of salvation entirely by
grace. For whilst some assert that good works are the cause of
justification; some that good works are united with the mer-
its of Christ and so both contribute to our justification; and
others that good works neither in whole nor in part justify,
but the act of faith; we renounce everything in point of our
acceptance with God, but his free Grace alone which justifies the ungodly, still treading in the steps of our venerable
forefathers, the compilers of the Baptist Confession of Faith,
who thus express themselves respecting the doctrine of justification: "Those whom God effectually calleth, he also freely
justifieth, . . . for Christ's sake alone; not by imputing faith
itself, the act of believing, or any other evangelical obedience
to them as their righteousness; but by imputing Christ's active
obedience unto the whole law, and passive obedience in his
death for their whole and sole righteousness, they receiving
and resting on him and his righteousness by faith" which "is
the alone instrument of justification."[18]

In this point do all the other lines of our confession meet.
For if it be admitted that justification is an act of free grace in
God without any respect to the merit or demerit of the person justified, then the doctrines of Jehovah's sovereign love in
choosing to himself a people from before the foundation of the
world, his sending his Son to expiate *their* guilt, his effectual
operations upon *their* hearts, and his perfecting the work he has
begun in them until those whom he justifies he also glorifies,
will be embraced as necessary parts of the glorious scheme of
our salvation.[19]

"I Came to Preach the Gospel"

One leading characteristic of Pearce's spirituality has already been
noted, namely, its crucicentrism. "Christ crucified," his good friend

---

[18] The Second London Confession of Faith 11.1, 2.
[19] Samuel Pearce, *The Doctrine of Salvation by Free Grace Alone* (1795; repr., n.p.: New York Baptist Association, 1855), 2.

Andrew Fuller wrote of him, "was his darling theme, from first to last."[20] A second prominent feature of his spirituality was a passion for the salvation of his fellow human beings. On a preaching trip to Wales, for instance, he wrote to his wife, Sarah Hopkins Pearce, about the lovely countryside that he was passing through: "Every pleasant scene which opened to us on our way (& they were very numerous) lost half its beauty because my lovely Sarah was not present to partake its pleasures with me." But, he added, "to see the Country was not the immediate object of my visiting Wales—I came to preach the gospel—to tell poor Sinners of the dear Lord Jesus—to endeavour to restore the children of misery to the pious pleasures of divine enjoyment."[21]

This evangelistic and missionary passion is strikingly revealed in four events.

"Doing . . . Good"

The first event took place when Pearce was asked to preach at the opening of a Baptist meetinghouse in Guilsborough, Northamptonshire, in May 1794. The previous meetinghouse had been burnt down at Christmas, 1792, by a mob that was hostile to Baptists. Pearce had spoken in the morning on Psalm 76:10 ("Surely the wrath of man shall praise thee: the remainder of wrath shalt thou restrain"—KJV). Later that day, during the midday meal, it was quite evident from the conversation around the dinner tables that Pearce's sermon had been warmly appreciated. It was thus no surprise when Pearce was asked if he would be willing to preach again the following morning. "If you will find a congregation," he responded, "I will find a sermon." It was agreed to have the sermon at 5:00 a.m. so that a number of farm laborers could come who wanted to hear Pearce preach and who would have to be at their tasks early in the morning.

---

[20] Fuller, *Memoirs of the Late Rev. Samuel Pearce* (2nd ed.), 140. For crucicentrism as a distinctive characteristic of eighteenth-century evangelicalism, see David Bebbington, *Evangelicalism in Modern Britain: A History from the 1730s to the 1980s* (1989; repr., Grand Rapids: Baker, 1992), 14–17.

[21] Samuel Pearce, letter to Sarah Pearce, July 11, 1792, Samuel Pearce Manuscripts, Angus Library, Regent's Park College, University of Oxford.

After Pearce had preached the second time, and that to a congregation of more than two hundred people, and he was sitting at breakfast with a few others, including Andrew Fuller, the latter remarked to Pearce how pleased he had been with the content of his friend's sermon. But, he went on to say, it seemed to him that Pearce's sermon was poorly structured. "I thought," Fuller told his friend, "you did not seem to close when you had really finished. I wondered that, contrary to what is usual with you, you seemed, as it were, to begin again at the end—how was it?" Pearce's response was terse: "It was so; but I had my reason." "Well then, come, let us have it," Fuller jovially responded. Pearce was quite reluctant to divulge the reason, but after a further entreaty from Fuller, he consented and said:

> Well, my brother, you shall have the secret, if it must be so.
> Just at the moment I was about to resume my seat, thinking
> I had finished, the door opened, and I saw a poor man enter,
> of the working class; and from the sweat on his brow, and the
> symptoms of his fatigue, I conjectured that he had walked some
> miles to this early service, but that he had been unable to reach
> the place till the close. A momentary thought glanced through
> my mind here may be a man who never heard the gospel,
> or it may be he is one that regards it as a feast of fat things;
> in either case, the effort on his part demands one on mine. So
> with the hope of doing him good, I resolved at once to forget all
> else, and, in despite of criticism, and the apprehension of being
> thought tedious, to give him a quarter of an hour.[22]

As Fuller and the others present at the breakfast table listened to this simple explanation, they were deeply impressed by Pearce's evident love for souls. Not afraid to appear as one lacking in homiletical skill, especially in the eyes of his fellow pastors, Pearce in his zeal for the spiritual health of *all* his hearers had sought to minister as best he could to this "poor man" who had arrived late.

---

[22] Cox, *History of the Baptist Missionary Society*, 1:52–53. Pearce's friendship with Fuller drew him into a highly significant circle of friends. For the story of this circle, see Michael A. G. Haykin, *One Heart and One Soul: John Sutcliff of Olney, His Friends and His Times* (Darlington, UK: Evangelical Press, 1995).

"An Instrument of Establishing the Empire of My Dear Lord"

Given his ardor for the advance of the gospel, it is only to be expected that Pearce would, in October 1792, be vitally involved in the formation of what would eventually be termed the Baptist Missionary Society, the womb of the modern missionary movement. Behind the formation of this missionary society lay nearly a decade of prayer that had been inspired by Jonathan Edwards's *Humble Attempt*. In the spring of 1784, an English Baptist pastor by the name of John Ryland Jr. (1753–1825), who would become a close friend of Samuel Pearce, shared with his two closest friends and fellow pastors, John Sutcliff (1752–1814) and Andrew Fuller, this treatise of Edwards that we considered in the previous chapter. It had been sent to him by the Scottish Presbyterian minister John Erskine (1721–1803).

When Erskine was in his midtwenties he had entered into correspondence with Edwards, and long after Edwards's death in 1758 Erskine had continued to uphold Edwards's theological perspectives and to heartily recommend his books. Well described as "the paradigm of Scottish evangelical missionary interest through the last half of the eighteenth century,"[23] Erskine regularly corresponded with Ryland from 1780 until the former's death in 1803, sending him not only letters, but also, on occasion, bundles of interesting books and tracts that he sought to promote. Thus it was in April 1784 that Erskine mailed to Ryland a copy of Edwards's *Humble Attempt*.

Reading Edwards's *Humble Attempt* in the spring of 1784 had a profound impact on Ryland, Fuller, and Sutcliff. As they met that June with other Baptist pastors at the annual meeting of the Northamptonshire Association, Sutcliff proposed that the churches of the association establish monthly prayer meetings for the outpouring of God's Holy Spirit and the consequent revival of the

---

[23] J. A. De Jong, *As the Waters Cover the Sea: Millennial Expectations in the Rise of Anglo-America Missions, 1640–1810* (Kampen: Kok, 1970), 166.

churches of Great Britain. This proposal was adopted by the representatives of the sixteen churches at the meeting, and on the last page of the circular letter sent out that year to the churches of the association there was a call for them "to wrestle with God for the effusion of His Holy Spirit."[24] After recommending that there be corporate prayer for one hour on the first Monday evening of the month, the call, most likely drawn up by Sutcliff, continued:

> The grand object in prayer is to be, that the Holy Spirit may be poured down on our ministers and churches, that sinners may be converted, the saints edified, the interest of religion revived, and the name of God glorified. At the same time remember, we trust you will not confine your requests to your own societies [i.e., churches] or to your own immediate connection [i.e., denomination]; let the whole interest of the Redeemer be affectionately remembered, and the spread of the gospel to the most distant parts of the habitable globe be the object of your most fervent requests. We shall rejoice if any other Christian societies of our own or other denomination will unite with us, and do now invite them most cordially to join heart and hand in the attempt.
>
> Who can tell what the consequences of such an united effort in prayer may be! Let us plead with God the many gracious promises of His word, which relate to the future success of His gospel. He has said, "I will yet for this be inquired of by the house of Israel, to do it for them, I will increase them with men like a flock" (Ezek. 36:37). Surely we have love enough for Zion to set apart one hour at a time, twelve times in a year, to seek her welfare.[25]

Noteworthy in this "Prayer Call" is its distinct missionary emphasis. The members of the association churches were urged to pray that the gospel be spread "to the most distant parts of the habitable globe." Little did these Baptists realize how God would

---

[24] Attached to the circular letter of the Northamptonshire Association, in John Ryland Jr., *The Nature, Evidences, and Advantages, of Humility* (Northamptonshire: T. Dicey, 1784), 12.
[25] Ibid.

begin to fulfill these very prayers within the space of less than a decade. God answered in two ways. First, by providing a man with the desire to go and evangelize peoples to whom the name of Christ was completely unknown, namely, William Carey.[26] And second, by giving other believers like Pearce the strength and courage to support him as he went and labored.

Over the next four decades Carey's example would spur numerous others to offer themselves for missionary service. One of the first was Pearce. By 1794 Pearce was so deeply gripped by the cause of missions that he had arrived at the conviction that he should offer his services to the society and go out to India to join the first missionary team the society had sent out, namely, Carey, John Thomas (1757–1801), and their respective families. Pearce began to study Bengali on his own.[27] And for the entire month of October 1794, which preceded the early November meeting of the society's administrative committee where Pearce's offer would be evaluated, Pearce set apart "one day in every week to secret prayer and fasting" for direction.[28] He also kept a diary of his experiences during this period, much of which Fuller later inserted verbatim into his *Memoirs* of Pearce and which admirably displays what Fuller described as his friend's "singular submissiveness to the will of God."[29]

During one of these days of prayer, fasting, and seeking God's face, Pearce recorded how God met with him in a remarkable way. Pearce had begun the day with "solemn prayer for the assistance of the Holy Spirit"[30] so that he might "enjoy the spirit and power of prayer" and have his "personal religion improved" and his "public steps directed."[31] He proceeded to read a portion of Edwards's life of

---

[26] For the details, see especially Timothy George, *Faithful Witness: The Life and Mission of William Carey* (Birmingham, AL: New Hope, 1991); and John Appleby, *"I can plod . . .": William Carey and the Early Years of the First Baptist Missionary Society* (London: Grace, 2007).

[27] Payne, "Samuel Pearce," 50.

[28] Fuller, *Memoirs of the Late Rev. Samuel Pearce* (2nd ed.), 38.

[29] Ibid., 59. For the diary, see 39–57. For some lengthy extracts from the diary, see also Michael A. G. Haykin, "Samuel Pearce, Extracts from a Diary: Calvinist Baptist Spirituality in the Eighteenth Century," *The Banner of Truth* 279 (December 1986): 9–18.

[30] Fuller, *Memoirs of the Late Rev. Samuel Pearce* (2nd ed.), 52.

[31] Ibid., 53.

David Brainerd, a book that quickened the zeal of many in Pearce's generation, and to peruse 2 Corinthians 2–6.[32] Afterward he went to prayer, but, he recorded, his heart was hard and "all was dullness," and he feared that somehow he had offended God.[33]

Suddenly, Pearce wrote, "it pleased God to smite the rock with the rod of his Spirit, and immediately the waters began to flow." Likening the frame of his heart to the rock in the desert that Moses struck with his rod in order to bring forth water (see Ex. 17:1–6), Pearce had found himself unable to generate any profound warmth for God and his dear cause. God, as it were, had to come by his Spirit, "touch" Pearce's heart, and so quicken his affections. He was overwhelmed, he wrote, by "a heavenly glorious melting power." He saw afresh "the love of a crucified Redeemer" and "the attractions of his cross." He felt, as he put it, "like Mary [Magdalene] at the master's feet weeping, for tenderness of soul; like a little child, for submission to my heavenly father's will."[34] The need to take the gospel to those who had never heard it gripped him anew "with an irresistible drawing of soul" and, again in his own words, "compelled me to vow that I would, by his leave, serve him among the heathen."[35] As he wrote later in his diary:

> If ever in my life I knew anything of the influences of the Holy Spirit, I did at this time. I was swallowed up in God. Hunger, fulness, cold, heat, friends and enemies, all seemed nothing before God. I was in a new world. All was delightful; for Christ was all, and in all. Many times I concluded prayer, but when rising from my knees, communion with God was so desirable, that I was sweetly drawn to it again and again, till my . . . strength was almost exhausted.[36]

The decision of the society as to Pearce's going overseas as a missionary was ultimately a negative one. When the executive commit-

[32] On the life of Brainerd, see chap. 5.
[33] Fuller, *Memoirs of the Late Rev. Samuel Pearce* (2nd ed.), 54.
[34] Ibid.
[35] Ibid., 55
[36] Ibid.

tee of the society met at Roade, Northamptonshire, on November 12, it was of the opinion that Pearce could best serve the cause of missions at home in England. His response to this decision is best seen in extracts from two letters. The first, written to his wife, Sarah, the day after he received the decision, stated: "I am disappointed, but not dismayed. I ever wish to make my Saviour's will my own."[37] The second, sent to Carey over four months later, contains a similar desire to submit to the perfectly good and sovereign will of God:

> Instead of a letter, you perhaps expected to have seen the writer; and had the will of God been so, he would by this time have been on his way to Mudnabatty: but it is not in man that walketh to direct his steps. Full of hope and expectation as I was, when I wrote you last, that I should be honoured with a mission to the poor heathen, and be an instrument of establishing the empire of my dear Lord in India, I must submit now to stand still, and see the salvation of God.

Pearce then told Carey some of the details of the November meeting at which the society executive had made their decision regarding his going overseas:

> I shall ever love my dear brethren the more for the tenderness with which they treated me, and the solemn prayer they repeatedly put up to God for me. At last, I withdrew for them to decide, and whilst I was apart from them, and engaged in prayer for divine direction, I felt all anxiety forsake me, and an entire resignation of will to the will of God, be it what it would, together with a satisfaction that so much praying breath would not be lost; but that He who hath promised to be found of all that seek him, would assuredly direct the hearts of my brethren to that which was most pleasing to himself, and most suitable to the interests of his kingdom in the world. Between two and

---

[37] Ibid., 35.

three hours were they deliberating after which time a paper was put into my hands, of which the following is a copy.

> The brethren at this meeting are fully satisfied of the fitness of brother P[earce]'s qualifications, and greatly approve of the disinterestedness of his motives and the ardour of his mind. But another Missionary not having been requested, and not being in our view immediately necessary, and brother P[earce] occupying already a post very important to the prosperity of the Mission itself, we are unanimously of opinion that at present, however, he should continue in the situation which he now occupies.

In response to this decision, which dashed some of Pearce's deepest longings, he was, he said, "enabled cheerfully to reply, 'The will of the Lord be done'; and receiving this answer as the voice of God, I have, for the most part, been easy since, though not without occasional pantings of spirit after the publishing of the gospel to the Pagans."[38]

From the perspective of the highly individualistic spirit of twenty-first-century Western Christianity, Pearce's friends seem to have been quite wrong in refusing to send him to India. If, during his month of fasting and prayer, he had felt he knew God's will for his life, was not the Baptist Missionary Society executive committee wrong in the decision they made? And should not Pearce have persisted in pressing his case for going? While these questions may seem natural to ask given the cultural matrix of contemporary Western Christianity, Pearce knew himself to be part of a team, and he was more interested in the triumph of that team's strategy than the fulfillment of his own personal desires.[39]

---

[38] Samuel Pearce, letter to William Carey, March 27, 1795, in *Missionary Correspondence: Containing Extracts of Letters from the Late Mr. Samuel Pearce, to the Missionaries in India, between the Years 1794, and 1798; and from Mr. John Thomas, from 1798, to 1800* (London: T. Gardiner, 1814), 26, 30–31.
[39] See Ralph D. Winter, "William Carey's Major Novelty," in *Carey's Obligation and India's Renaissance*, ed. J. T. K. Daniel and R. E. Hedlund (Serampore, West Bengal: Council of Serampore College, 1993), 136–37.

"Surely Irish Zion Demands Our Prayers"

Pearce's passion for the lost found outlet in other ways, though. In July 1795 he received an invitation from the General Evangelical Society in Dublin to come over to Dublin and preach at a number of venues. He was not able to go until the following year, when he left Birmingham at 8:00 a.m. on May 31. After traveling through Wales and taking passage on a ship from Holyhead, he landed in Dublin on Saturday afternoon, June 4.[40] Pearce stayed with a Presbyterian elder by the name of Hutton, who was a member of a congregation pastored by a Dr. McDowell.[41] Pearce preached to this congregation on a number of occasions, as well as other congregations in the city, including the Baptists.

Baptist witness in Dublin went back to the Cromwellian era and 1653, when through the ministry of Thomas Patient (d. 1666), the first Calvinistic Baptist meetinghouse was built in Swift's Alley.[42] The church grew rapidly at first, and by 1725 it had between 150 and 200 members.[43] A new meetinghouse was put up in the 1730s. By the time Pearce came to Ireland in 1796, though, the membership had declined to roughly forty members. Pearce's impressions of the congregation were not very positive. In a letter he wrote to Carey in August 1796, the month after returning to England, he told the missionary:

> There were 10 Baptist societies in Ireland.—They are now reduced to 6 & bid fair soon to be perfectly extinct.
>
>   When I came to Dublin they had no meeting of any kind for religious purposes. . . . Indeed they were so dead to piety that, tho' of their own denomination, I saw & knew less of them than of every other professors in the place.[44]

---

[40] Samuel Pearce, letter to Sarah Pearce, June 4, 1796, Samuel Pearce Manuscripts.

[41] Ibid.

[42] B. R. White, "Thomas Patient in England and Ireland," *Irish Baptist Historical Society Journal* 2 (1969–1970): 41. See also Robert Dunlop, "Dublin Baptists from 1650 Onwards," *Irish Baptist Historical Society Journal* 21 (1988–1989): 6–7.

[43] Joshua Thompson, "Baptists in Ireland 1792–1922: A Dimension of Protestant Dissent" (DPhil diss., Regent's Park College, University of Oxford, 1988), 9.

[44] Samuel Pearce, letter to William Carey, August 1796, Samuel Pearce Carey Collection—Pearce Family Letters, Angus Library, Regent's Park College, University of Oxford.

This opinion does not appear to have dampened his zeal in preaching. A Dublin deacon wrote to a friend: "We have had a Jubilee for weeks. That blessed man of God, Samuel Pearce, has preached amongst us with great sweetness and much power."[45] And in a letter to his close friend Summers, Pearce acknowledged: "Never have I been more deeply taught my own nothingness; never has the power of God more evidently rested upon me. The harvest here is great indeed; and the Lord of the harvest has enabled me to labor in it with delight."[46] This passionate concern for the advance of the gospel in Ireland is well caught in a sentence from one of his letters to his wife, Sarah. "Surely," he wrote to her on June 24, "*Irish* Zion demands our prayers."[47]

"Who Can Tell What God Might Do"

In the three remaining years of Pearce's earthly life, he expended much of his energy in raising support for the cause of foreign missions. As he informed Carey in the fall of 1797:

> I can hardly refrain from repeating what I have so often told you before, that I long to meet you on earth and to join you in your labours of love among the poor dear heathens. Yes, would my Lord bid me so, I should with transport obey the summons and take a joyful farewell of the land that bare me, though it were for ever. But I must confess that the path of duty appears to me clearer than before to be at home, at least for the present. Not that I think my connexions in England a sufficient argument, but that I am somewhat necessary to the Mission itself, and shall be as long as money is wanted and our number of active friends does not increase. Brother Fuller and myself have the whole of the collecting business on our hands, and though there are many others about us who exceed me in grace and gifts, yet their other engagements forbid or their peculiar turn of mind disqualifies them for that kind

---

[45] Carey, *Samuel Pearce*, 119.

[46] *Memoir of Rev. Samuel Pearce. A.M.* (New York: American Tract Society, n.d.), 132.

[47] Samuel Pearce, letter to Sarah Pearce, June 24, 1796, Samuel Pearce Manuscripts.

of service. I wish, however, to be thankful if our dear Lord will but employ me as a foot in the body. I consider myself as united to the hands and eyes, and mouth, and heart, and all; and when the body rejoices, I have my share of gladness with the other members.[48]

One of the meetings at which Pearce preached was the one that saw William Ward (1769–1823)—later to be an invaluable coworker of Carey in India—accepted as a missionary with the Baptist Missionary Society. Those attending the meeting, which took place at Kettering on October 16, 1798, were deeply stirred by Pearce's passion and concern for the advance of the gospel. He preached "like an Apostle," Fuller later wrote to Carey. And when Ward wrote to Carey, he told his future colleague that Pearce "set the whole meeting in a flame. Had missionaries been needed, we might have had a cargo immediately."[49]

Returning back to Birmingham from this meeting, Pearce was caught in a heavy downpour, became drenched to the skin, and subsequently developed a severe chill. Neglecting to rest and foolishly thinking what he called "pulpit sweats" would effect a cure, he continued a rigorous schedule of preaching at Cannon Street, as well as in outlying villages around Birmingham. His lungs became so inflamed that Pearce had to ask Ward to supply the Cannon Street pulpit for a few months during the winter of 1798–1799. By mid-December 1798, Pearce could not converse for more than a few minutes without losing his breath. Yet still he was thinking of the salvation of the lost. Writing to Carey around this time, he told him of a plan he had been mulling over in his mind to take the gospel to France.

At that time Great Britain and France were locked in a titanic war, the Napoleonic War, which would last into the middle of the

---

[48] Samuel Pearce, letter to William Carey, September 8, 1797, in *Missionary Correspondence*, 53–54.

[49] Andrew Fuller, letter to William Carey, April 18, 1799, Letters of Andrew Fuller, typescript transcript, Angus Library, Regent's Park College, University of Oxford; William Ward, letter to William Carey, October 1798, quoted by S. Pearce Carey, *William Carey*, ed. Peter Masters (London: Wakeman Trust, 1993), 172. In his memoirs of Pearce, Fuller wrote that Pearce's sermon was "full of a holy unction, and seemed to breathe an apostolical ardour." *Memoirs of the Late Rev. Samuel Pearce* (2nd ed.), 100.

second decade of the next century. This war was the final and cli-
mactic episode in a struggle that had dominated the eighteenth
century. France and Great Britain had fought each other in wars in
every decade but one since the 1690s. Not surprisingly, there was
little love lost between the British and the French. For example,
Samuel Carter Hall (1800–1889), a man of letters, recalled one of his
earliest memories as a young boy when his father would put him on
his knee and give him three pieces of advice: "Be a good boy, love
your mother, and hate the French"![50] But Pearce was gripped by a
far different passion than those which gripped many in Britain and
France—his was the priority of the kingdom of Christ.

In one of the last sermons that he ever preached, on a day of
public thanksgiving for Horatio Nelson's victory over the French
Fleet at the Battle of the Nile (1798) and the repulse of a French
invasion fleet off the coast of Ireland in the fall of 1799, Pearce
pointedly said:

> Should any one expect that I shall introduce the *destruction* of
> our foes, by the late victories gained off the coasts of Egypt
> and Ireland, as the object of pleasure and gratitude, he will be
> disappointed. The man who can take pleasure at the destruc-
> tion of his fellow men, is a cannibal at heart; . . . but to the
> heart of him who calls himself a disciple of the merciful Jesus,
> let such pleasure be an everlasting stranger. Since in that sacred
> volume, which I revere as the fair gift of heaven to man, I am
> taught, that "of one blood God hath made all nations," [Acts
> 17:26] it is impossible for me not to regard every man as my
> brother, and to consider, that national differences ought not to
> excite personal animosities.[51]

A few months later—when he was desperately ill—he wrote a letter to Carey telling him of his plans for a missionary journey to
France. "I have been endeavouring for some years," he told Carey,

---

[50] Samuel Carter Hall, *Retrospect of a Long Life: From 1815 to 1883* (New York: D. Appleton, 1883), 45.
[51] Samuel Pearce, *Motives to Gratitude* (Birmingham, UK: James Belcher, 1798), 18–19.

to get five of our Ministers to agree that they will apply themselves to the French language, . . . then we [for he was obviously intending to be one of the five] might spend two months
annually in that Country, and at least satisfy ourselves that
Christianity was not lost in France for want of a fair experiment
in its favour: and who can tell what God might do![52]

God would use British evangelicals, notably Pearce's Baptist contemporary Robert Haldane (1764–1842), to take the gospel to
Francophones on the Continent when peace eventually came, but
Pearce's anointed preaching would play no part in that great work.
Yet his ardent prayers on behalf of the French could not have been
without some effect. Prayers for the conversion of the unsaved are
never lost.

By the spring of 1799 Pearce was desperately ill with pulmonary
tuberculosis. By the time he wrote the above letter to Carey, his
voice was so far gone that he could not even whisper without pain
in his lungs. His suffering, though, seemed to act like a refiner's fire
to draw him closer to Christ. "Blessed be his dear name," he said
not long before his death,

who shed his blood for me. . . . Now I see the value of the religion of the cross. It is a religion for a dying sinner. . . . Yes,
I taste its sweetness, and enjoy its fulness, with all the gloom
of a dying-bed before me; and far rather would I be the poor
emaciated and emaciating creature that I am, than be an emperor with every earthly good about him, but without a God.[53]

Pearce fell asleep in Christ on Thursday, October 10, 1799. He
left unfinished a comprehensive history of missions that he had
been working on, which undoubtedly would have traced some of
the line of Calvinistic mission that we have examined in this book.
Ward, who had been profoundly influenced by Pearce's zeal and
spirituality and who spent the strength of his life on the mission

[52] Quoted by Carey, *Samuel Pearce*, 189.
[53] Fuller, *Memoirs of the Late Rev. Samuel Pearce* (2nd ed.), 141.

field in India with Carey, well summed up Pearce's character when he wrote not long before the latter's death:

> Oh, how does personal religion shine in Pearce! What a soul! What ardour for the glory of God! . . . you see in him a mind wholly given up to God; a sacred lustre shines in his conversation: always tranquil, always cheerful. . . . I have seen more of God in him than in any other person I ever met.[54]

The Lesson of Pearce's Life for Calvinists

A central aim of this book has been to demonstrate that there is a Calvinistic tradition of missionary passion that goes back from pioneers of the modern missionary movement, like Carey and Pearce, through the Puritans to the Reformed fountainhead in the writings and labors of John Calvin and, as such, puts to rest the myth that one cannot be both Calvinistic and missional. But this book is also a call to those who rejoice in their Calvinism to be sure that they are equally passionate about missions and evangelism. Oh, that Pearce's example—his zeal to see the lost won to Christ and truly converted, "his so remarkable devoting himself and his all, in heart and practice, to the glory of God, . . . may excite in us all . . . a due sense of the greatness of the [missional] work we have to do in this world."[55]

---

[54] Quoted by Carey, *Samuel Pearce*, 188.

[55] These words are taken appropriately from Jonathan Edwards's conclusion to his funeral sermon for David Brainerd: *A Sermon Preached on the Day of the Funeral of the Rev. Mr. David Brainerd*, in *The Life of David Brainerd*, ed. Norman Pettit, vol. 7 of *The Works of Jonathan Edwards* (New Haven, CT: Yale University Press, 1985), 553–54.

Selected Bibliography of Secondary Literature

Accardy, Chris. "Calvin's Ministry to the Waldensians." *Reformation and Revival* 10, no. 4 (Fall 2001): 45–58.

Baez-Camargo, G. "The Earliest Protestant Missionary Venture in Latin America." *Church History* 21 (June 1952): 135–45.

Barro, Antonio Carlos. "Election, Predestination and the Mission of God." In *John Calvin and Evangelical Theology: Legacy and Prospect. In Celebration of the Quincentenary of John Calvin*, edited by Sung Wook Chung, 181–98. Louisville, KY: Westminster John Knox, 2009.

Beaver, R. Pierce. "The Genevan Mission to Brazil." In *The Heritage of John Calvin*, edited by John H. Bratt, 55–73. Grand Rapids: Eerdmans, 1973.

Bebbington, David W. *Evangelicalism in Modern Britain: A History from the 1730s to the 1980s*. 1989. Reprint, Grand Rapids: Baker, 1992.

Beeke, Joel R. "John Calvin: Teacher and Practitioner of Evangelism." *Reformation and Revival* 10, no. 4 (Fall 2001): 107–19.

Berthoud, Jean-Marc. "John Calvin and the Spread of the Gospel in France." In *Fulfilling the Great Commission*. Westminster Conference Papers, 1–53. London: Westminster Conference, 1992.

Bosch, David J. *Transforming Mission: Paradigm Shifts in Theology of Mission*. Marynoll, NY: Orbis, 1991.

Buckler, Andrew. *Jean Calvin et la mission de l'Eglise*. Lyon: Editions Olivétan, 2008.

Calhoun, David B. "John Calvin: Missionary Hero or Missionary Failure?" *Presbyterion* 5 (Spring 1979): 16–33.

Chaney, Charles. "The Missionary Dynamic in the Theology of John Calvin." *The Reformed Review* 17 (March 1964): 24–38.

Coates, Thomas. "Were the Reformers Mission-Minded?" *Concordia Theological Monthly* 40 (October 1969): 600–611.

Cogley, Richard W. *John Eliot's Mission to the Indians before King Philip's War*. Cambridge, MA: Harvard University Press, 1999.

———. "John Eliot's Puritan Ministry." *Fides et Historia* 31, no. 1 (1999): 1–18.

Collier, Hugh. "John Eliot—Apostle to the Indians." *Reformation Trust* 254 (July–August 2013): 17–21.

Davies, Ronald E. "The Great Commission from Calvin to Carey." *Evangel* 14 (Summer 1996): 44–49.

———. *A Heart for Mission: Five Pioneer Thinkers*. Fearn, Tain, Rossshire: Christian Focus, 2002.

———. "Jonathan Edwards: Missionary Biographer, Theologian, Strategist, Administrator, Advocate—and Missionary." *International Bulletin of Missionary Research* 21, no. 2 (April 1997): 60–67.

———. "Jonathan Edwards, Theologian of the Missionary Awakening." *EMA Occasional Paper* 3 (Spring 1999). *Evangel* 17, no. 1 (Spring 1999): 1–8.

———. "Prepare Ye the Way of the Lord: The Missiological Thought and Practice of Jonathan Edwards (1703–1758)." PhD thesis, Fuller Theological Seminary, 1989.

Edwards, Charles E. "Calvin and Mission." *The Evangelical Quarterly* 8 (1936): 47–51.

Fry, C. George. "John Calvin: Theologian and Evangelist." *Christianity Today* 15, no. 2 (October 23, 1970): 3–6.

Gibson, Jonathan. "Jonathan Edwards: A *Missionary*?" *Themelios* 36 (2011): 380–402.

Gensichen, D. H.-W. "Were the Reformers Indifferent to Missions?" In *History's Lessons for Tomorrow's Mission: Milestones in the History of Missionary Thinking*, edited by Audrey Abrecht, 119–27. Geneva: World's Student Christian Federation. 1960.

Gordon, Amy Glassner. "The First Protestant Missionary Effort: Why Did It Fail?" *International Bulletin of Missionary Research* 8, no. 1 (January 1984): 12–18.

Gordon, Bruce. *Calvin*. New Haven, CT: Yale University Press, 2009.

Haykin, Michael A. G. "Calvin on Missions." *The Founders Journal* 75 (Winter 2009): 20–27.

———. "John Calvin's Missionary Influence in France." *Reformation and Revival* 10, no. 4 (Fall 2001): 34–44.

———. *Joy Unspeakable and Full of Glory: The Piety of Samuel and Sarah Pearce*. Kitchener, ON: Joshua, 2012.

———. *One Heart and One Soul: John Sutcliff of Olney, His Friends and His Times*. Darlington, County Durham: Evangelical Press, 1994.

———. "'A Sacrifice Well Pleasing to God': John Calvin and the Missionary Endeavor of the Church." *The Southern Baptist Journal of Theology* 13, no. 4 (Winter 2009): 36–43.

———. "'A Sacrifice Well Pleasing to God': John Calvin and the Missionary Endeavors of the Church." *The Banner of Sovereign Grace Truth* 17, no. 1 (January 2009): 7–9.

Hendrix, Scott. "Rerooting the Faith: The Reformation as Re-Christianization." *Church History* 69 (2000): 558–77.

Hinkinson, Jon. "Missions among Puritans and Pietists." In *The Great Commission: Evangelicals and the History of World Missions*, edited by Martin I. Klauber and Scott M. Manetsch, 23–34. Nashville, TN: B&H, 2008.

Hughes, Philip Edgcumbe. "John Calvin: Director of Missions." In *The Heritage of John Calvin*, edited by John H. Bratt, 40–54. Grand Rapids: Eerdmans, 1973.

Marsden, George M. "Jonathan Edwards, the Missionary." *Journal of Presbyterian History* 81, no. 1 (Spring 2003): 5–17.

McKee, Elsie. "Calvin and Praying for 'All People Who Dwell on Earth.'" *Interpretation* 63, no. 2 (April 2009): 130–40.

Morris, S. L. "The Relation of Calvin and Calvinism to Missions." In *Calvin Memorial Addresses*, edited by Benjamin B. Warfield, Richard Reed, James Orr, R. A. Webb, and Thomas Cary Johnson, 127–46. 1909. Reprint, Birmingham, AL: Solid Ground Christian Books, 2007.

Nichols, Stephen J. "Last of the Mohican Missionaries: Jonathan Edwards at Stockbridge." In *The Legacy of Jonathan Edwards: American Religion and the Evangelical Tradition*, edited by D. G. Hart, Sean Michael Lucas, and Stephen J. Nichols, 47–63. Grand Rapids: Baker, 2003.

Packer, J. I. "Puritan Evangelism." In *A Quest for Godliness: The Puritan Vision of the Christian Life*, 291–308. Wheaton, IL: Crossway, 1990.

Parsons, Michael. *Calvin's Preaching on the Prophet Micah: The 1550–1551 Sermons in Geneva*. Lewiston, NY: Edwin Mellen, 2006.

Reid, W. Stanford. "Calvin's Geneva: A Missionary Centre." *The Reformed Theological Review* 42, no. 3 (September–December 1983): 65–74.

Rogers, Mark C. "A Missional Eschatology: Jonathan Edwards, Future Prophecy, and the Spread of the Gospel." *Fides et Historia* 41, no. 1 (Winter/Spring 2009): 23–46.

Rooy, Sidney H. *The Theology of Missions in the Puritan Tradition*. 1965. Reprint, Laurel, MS: Audubon, 2006.

Stanley, Brian. "Christian Missions and the Enlightenment: A Reevaluation." In *Christian Missions and the Enlightenment*, edited by Brian Stanley, 1–21. Grand Rapids: Eerdmans, 2001.

Stewart, Kenneth J. "Calvinism and Missions: The Contested Relationship Revisited." *Themelios* 34, no. 1 (April 2009): 63–78.

———. *Ten Myths about Calvinism: Recovering the Breadth of the Reformed Tradition*. Downers Grove, IL: InterVarsity, 2011.

Van den Berg, J. "Calvin's Missionary Message: Some Remarks about the Relation between Calvinism and Missions." *The Evangelical Quarterly* 22 (1950): 174–87.

Wallace, Dewey D., Jr. *The Spirituality of the Later English Puritans: An Anthology.* Macon, GA: Mercer University Press, 1987.

Walls, Andrew F. "The Eighteenth-Century Protestant Missionary Awakening in Its European Context." In *Christian Missions and the Enlightenment*, edited by Brian Stanley, 22–44. Grand Rapids: Eerdmans, 2001.

Weaver, G. Stephen, Jr. "A Seventeenth Century Baptist View of Ministry as Seen in Three Funeral Sermons by John Piggott." Unpublished paper, August 2006.

Wilcox, Pete. "Evangelization in the Thought and Practice of John Calvin." *Anvil: An Anglican Evangelical Journal for Theology and Mission* 12 (1995): 201–17.

General Index

Scripture Index

Also Available from
Michael A. G. Haykin

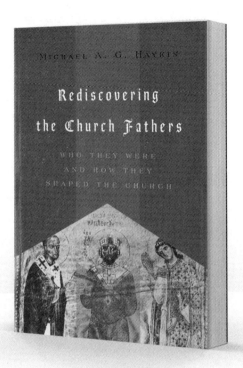

An organized and convenient introduction to the church fathers from AD 100 to 500. Haykin surveys a number of church fathers, outlining their roles in church history and their teaching on a number of topics.

"A user-friendly introduction to the early centuries of the Christian church. Everyone needs to know about these things, and this book is a great place to begin."

GERALD BRAY, *Research Professor of Divinity, Beeson Divinity School*

"This introduction by an eminent evangelical scholar opens the door to the riches of early Christianity for evangelicals in a splendidly concise handbook of sorts. Evangelicals, who are experiencing a renaissance of interest in the Fathers, need look no further than this volume for an introduction to many of the most significant figures in Christian history."

STEVEN A. MCKINION, *Professor of Theology and Patristics, Southeastern Baptist Theological Seminary, Wake Forest, North Carolina*